AF576725

THE NATIONAL GALLERY SCHOOLS OF PAINTING

French Paintings after 1800

THE NATIONAL GALLERY SCHOOLS OF PAINTING

French Paintings

after 1800

MICHAEL WILSON

Deputy Keeper, The National Gallery

The National Gallery, London,
in association with William Collins 1983

William Collins Sons & Co Ltd
London · Glasgow · Sydney · Auckland
Toronto · Johannesburg

British Library Cataloguing in Publication Data

Wilson, Michael, 1951–
French paintings after 1800.
1. Painting, French—Exhibitions
2. Painting, Modern—19th century—France—
Exhibitions.
I. Title
759.4′074 ND547

ISBN 0-00-217149-X
ISBN 0-00-217150-3 Pbk

First published 1983

Photoset in Imprint
by Ace Filmsetting Ltd, Frome, Somerset
Colour reproduction by
P.J. Graphics Ltd, London W3 8DH
Made and printed by
Staples Printers, Kettering, Ltd

Front cover shows a detail from *Bathers at La Grenouillère* by Monet

Back cover shows *Still-life with Apples and Pomegranate* by Courbet.

THE NATIONAL GALLERY SCHOOLS OF PAINTING

This series, published by William Collins in association with the National Gallery, offers the general reader an illustrated guide to all the schools of painting represented at the Gallery. Each volume contains fifty colour plates with a commentary by a member of the Gallery staff and a short introduction. The first three volumes in the series are:

Dutch Paintings by Christopher Brown
French Paintings after 1800 by Michael Wilson
Spanish and Later Italian Paintings by Michael Helston

Further volumes completing the series are due to be published in 1984 and 1985.

French Paintings after 1800

The nineteenth-century French rooms at the National Gallery contain some of the most popular paintings in the entire Collection: Manet's *Music in the Tuileries Gardens*, *La Première Sortie* by Renoir, Van Gogh's *Sunflowers*, the late *Water Lilies* by Monet and many more.

Impressionist and Post-Impressionist paintings such as these seem so accessible and full of joy that it is hard to imagine how they were long regarded as outside the bounds of art, and having no place in a public gallery. Native chauvinism meant that the National Gallery was particularly slow in recognizing the merits of nineteenth-century French painting and, in numbers at least, the Collection is still not strong in this field. Nevertheless, an active purchasing policy has in recent years redressed the balance, and as the plates in this book show the Collection now contains treasures of all kinds from the period.

The setting up in 1923 of the Courtauld Fund for the purchase of 'modern' French paintings, following soon after the bequest of Sir Hugh Lane's nineteenth-century paintings, established the basis of the Impressionist Collection. Twenty-two paintings were acquired, including works by Manet, Degas, Renoir, Pissarro and Seurat and all four Van Goghs belonging to the Gallery. Since then pictures by prominent artists not previously represented at all have been added – an important jungle subject by 'le douanier' Rousseau; a large religious painting by the symbolist Gustave Moreau; a pastel by Odilon Redon; a cubist still-life by Picasso; and an early portrait by Matisse.

With the growth of the Collection it is now possible to appreciate the diversity of nineteenth-century French painting, from Ingres' idealized portraits to Millet's forthright portrayals of peasant life and Degas' dancers, acrobats and bathers, from the historical subjects of Delacroix and Delaroche to the landscape 'motifs' of Monet, Pissarro and Cézanne. The century as a whole can be seen as one of astonishing contrasts and transitions, alive with experiment and great achievements.

MICHAEL WILSON is Deputy Keeper of the National Gallery in charge of French paintings. He has published two previous books on the National Gallery as well as *Eighteenth Century French Painting* and a book on Odilon Redon, *Nature and Imagination.*

Introduction

If asked to name the chief glories of the National Gallery, a typical visitor would probably mention the Italian schools, particularly the rare group of Pieros, the Ucello *Battle of San Romano*, the Raphaels, and the great paintings of the Venetian High Renaissance. He might also think of Rembrandt and Rubens (the Gallery has twenty-one paintings by each of them) and Claude and Poussin, both of whom are well represented. In contrast only a handful of rooms are devoted to nineteenth-century French painting, in spite of its popularity and the increased efforts on the part of the Gallery in recent years to make up the deficiency. Some visitors still express surprise to find Cézanne and Seurat at the National Gallery at all, a place that is irrevocably associated in most minds with Old Master Art. We thought that these artists were at the Tate, they say. Until well after the middle of this century most of the nation's French Impressionist and Post-Impressionist paintings were housed at the Tate Gallery as part of the Modern Foreign Collection, and some are still retained there as a prologue to the Modern rooms. But while the nineteenth-century French painters are now rightly hung beside their great predecessors at Trafalgar Square, they still make a slight showing beside the Italians and the Dutch. Not that anyone would dispute the masterpiece status of Ingres' *Madame Moitessier* (Plate No. 8) or Seurat's *Bathers* (Plate No. 31) or Van Gogh's *Sunflowers* (Plate No. 35). Yet in numbers the group still must count as comparatively weak. Beside the large holdings of Botticelli, Titian, Ruisdael and Teniers, we can boast only a handful of works by Delacroix, Ingres and Millet. Géricault, Daumier, Sisley, Seurat, Gauguin, Moreau and Redon are represented by only one painting apiece. And the Gallery has nothing by Jacques-Louis David at one end of the century or Bonnard at the other.

The situation at the National Gallery, however, is not untypical of the country as a whole. Public and private collections in England are wealthy in Old Master painting, and in general abysmally weak in foreign nineteenth- and twentieth-century art. The reasons are historical and do the country little credit. While collectors in Europe and America grasped at an early date the lead that France had taken in painting in the nineteenth century, and recognized in turn the innovations wrought by Delacroix, the Barbizon school, the Realists, the Impressionists and their successors, the English remained contemptuously dismissive of any contemporary art that did not originate within their own shores. And while American and German collectors eagerly bought the modern French art of the period, the English turned their backs on what, in the words of one English critic, 'connoted lubricity, bloodshed and a pursuit of the ugly'.

The Revolution had undoubtedly earned France the lasting distrust of the English. To the crimes of Popery and immorality it had added irreligion and political subversiveness. Nevertheless a stream of major French painters made profitable contacts with England during the century. Géricault and Delacroix both visited England in the 1820s and were enormously enthusiastic about British art. After the middle of the century Daubigny, Fantin-Latour and Manet followed suit and hoped to benefit from their new contacts. During a short stay in London in July 1868 Manet wrote to Fantin-Latour, 'I have been enchanted by London and by the good reception I have received from everyone with whom I have been.' But his hopes for a one-man show came to nothing and in spite of the presence of his friends Whistler and Alphonse Legros in the capital, he found no one prepared to buy his work.

Monet, Pissarro and Sisley all took refuge in England during the Franco-Prussian War of 1870–71 and were so pleased by what they saw, particularly of London and its environs, that they each returned in later years and produced some of their finest work of English subjects. 'Monet and I were very enthusiastic over the London landscapes,' Pissarro later recalled. But their paintings were rejected by the Royal Academy and in May 1871 Pissarro wrote to Théodore Duret from London completely disillusioned with the city. 'It is only abroad that one feels how beautiful, great and hospitable France is. What a difference here! One gathers only contempt, indifference, even rudeness; among colleagues there is the most egotistical jealousy and resentment. Here there is no art; everything is a question of business. As far as my private affairs, sales, are concerned, I've done nothing, except with Durand-Ruel, who bought two small pictures from me. My painting doesn't catch on, not at all; this follows me more or less everywhere.' In spite of Pissarro's feelings, his son Lucien, a painter also, later followed him to England and in 1890 settled there. As for Sisley, he had English relatives, but they disapproved of his painting and offered him no support.

It was in London that Monet and Pissarro were introduced by

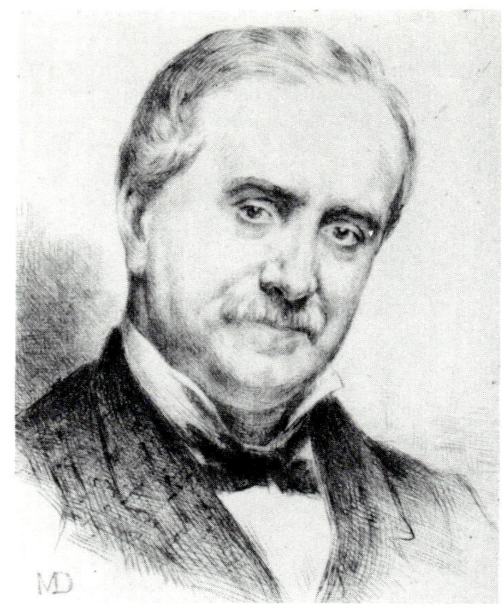

Portrait of Paul Durand-Ruel *by Marcellin Desboutin. 1882. Paris, Bibliothèque Nationale, Cabinet des Estampes.*

L'Absinthe *by Edgar Degas. 1876. Paris. Musée du Louvre, Galerie du Jeu de Paume.*

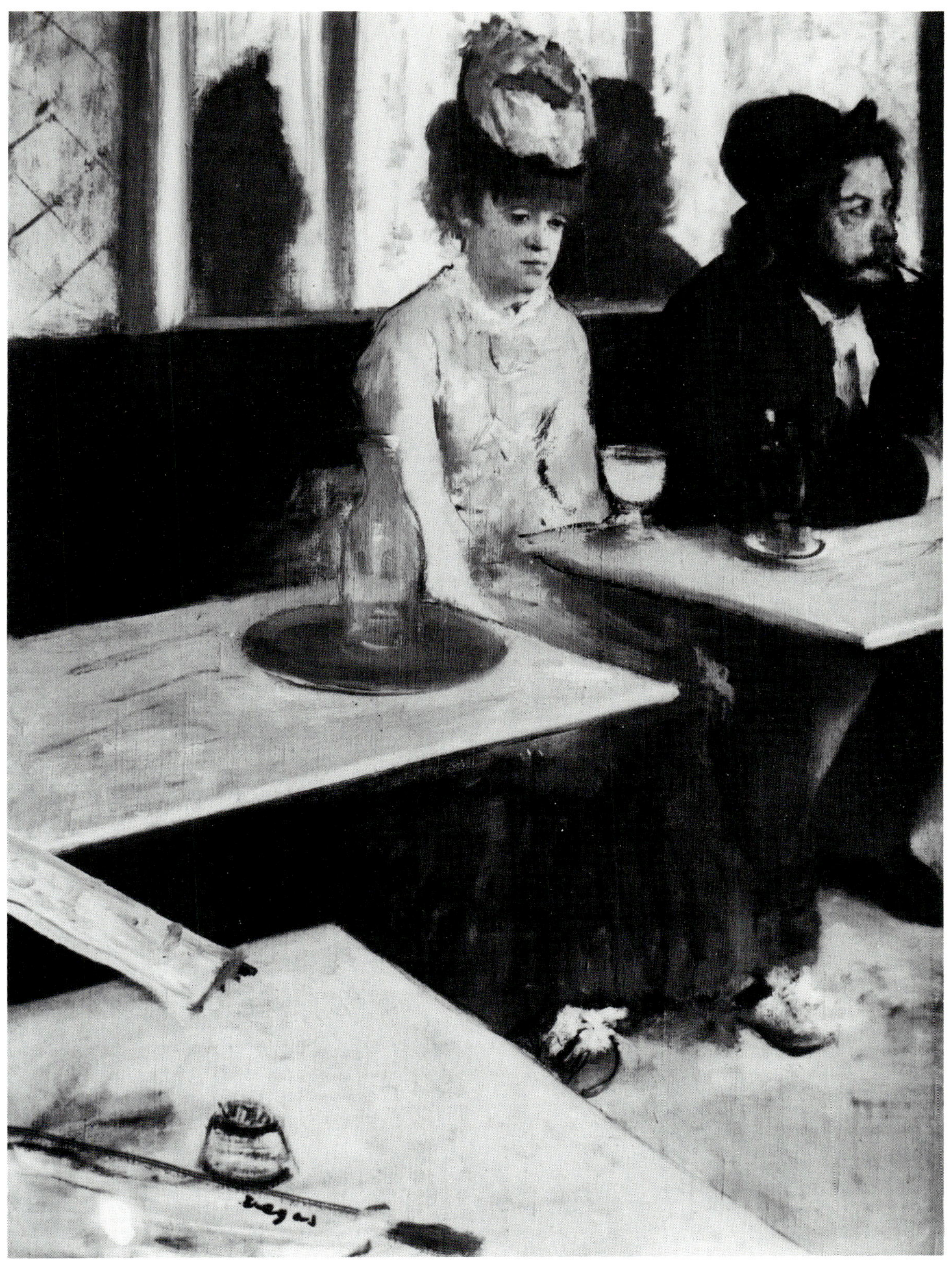
Degas

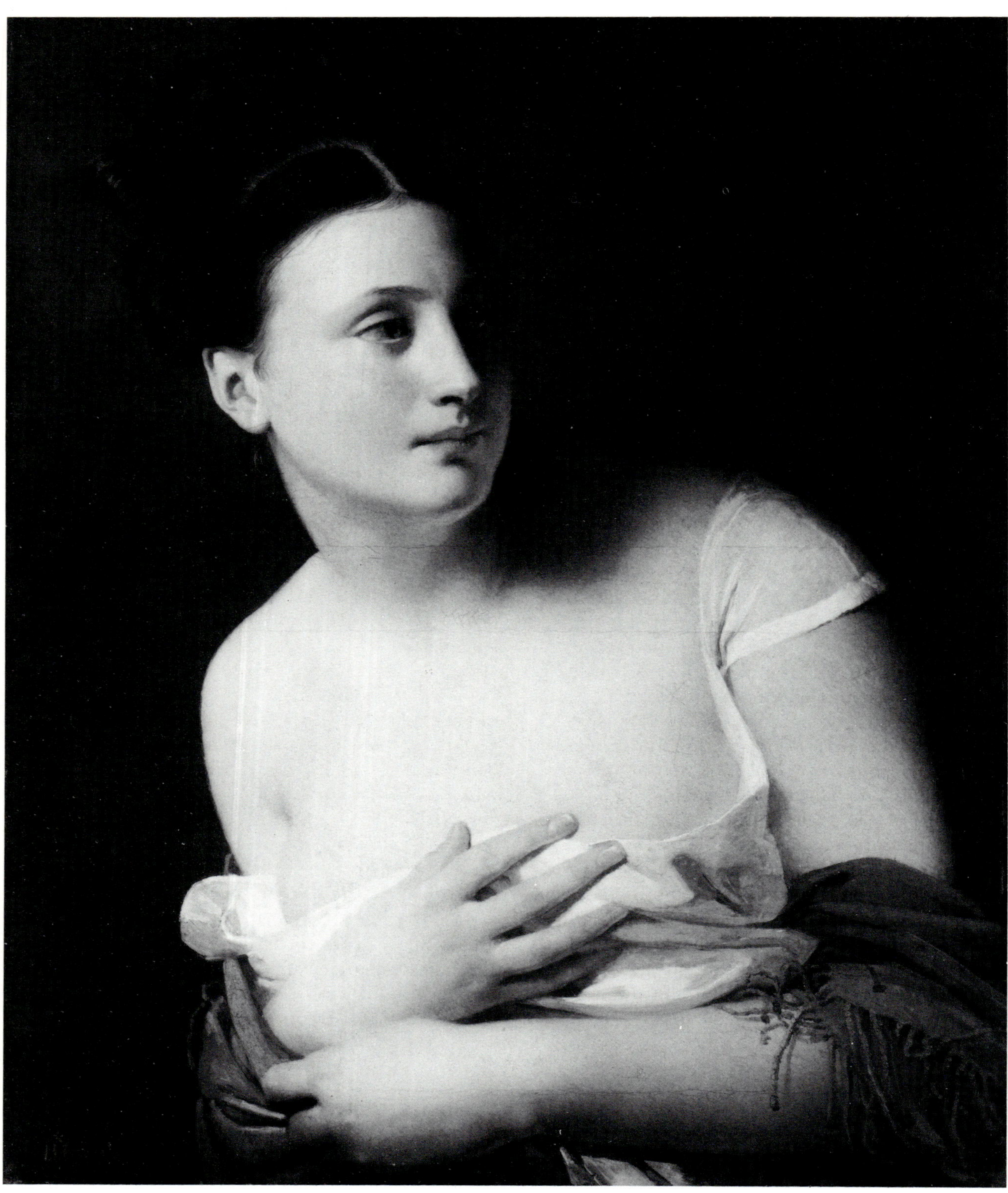

The Surprise *by Claude-Marie Dubufe. This was the first painting by a foreign nineteenth-century artist to enter the Collection. It formed part of the Robert Vernon Gift, 1847.*

Daubigny to the dealer Paul Durand-Ruel. As he had taken up the Barbizon painters years before and championed them in the face of hostile criticism until he won a market for them, so he bravely purchased works by the as yet unknown (and unnamed) Impressionists. The story of Durand-Ruel's brave support during years of indifference is well-known. In France during the 1880s critics and collectors were gradually won over by his efforts to promote the new movement, and in 1886 Durand-Ruel had a notable triumph with the exhibition he sent to New York, thus opening the American market. But in England he met with no similar success. Between 1870 and 1875 he mounted no fewer than ten exhibitions of French art in his Bond Street Gallery without making any impact on the obdurate London public, and in 1882 and 1883, when he returned with exhibitions of Impressionist painting, he still met with incomprehension.

It was not that the critics and the public failed to recognize the innovations made by Monet, Renoir, Degas and their colleagues in the treatment of light and the use of colour, but that their critical preconceptions blinkered them to the quality of the paintings. Contemporary taste found them too bright, too sketchy and lacking the conventional element of 'beauty' considered necessary to a work of art. As the critic of the *Illustrated London News* succinctly put it, 'The more extravagant of the examples shown greatly shock, by their slightness, roughness and violent contrasts of bright light and blue shadows . . . But the great fault of the French Impressionists is their perverse disregard of or insensibility to beauty, especially in form.' It is hardly surprising that while English painters pandered to the popular taste for genre paintings with a Greco-Roman flavour – particularly scenes of everyday life in ancient times, executed with a slick illusionism that passed for excellence – critics should have found the subject matter of the Impressionists vulgar and ugly. The attitude of the public is well illustrated by the account of the reception of Degas' famous painting popularly known as *L'Absinthe* which is today in the Louvre. When it appeared in a London saleroom in 1892 it was hissed at, and when the following year it was exhibited at the Grafton Gallery, it became the subject of a heated controversy. While a small band of *avant garde* artists and critics defended the picture, it was variously described in the press as 'vulgar', 'boozy', 'sottish', 'loathsome', 'revolting', 'ugly', 'degraded' and 'repulsive'.

In view of these sentiments, it is hardly surprising, though still shocking, to learn that by 1900 the National Gallery Collection contained only seven paintings by foreign nineteenth-century painters, and that these were all acquired as gifts or bequests. Their acceptance did not require courage as none of the artists concerned was a challenge to conventional taste. Claude-Marie Dubufe, Rosa Bonheur, Pierre-Charles Poussin, Charles-Philogène Tschaggeny, Paul Jean Clays, Josephus Laurentius Dyckmans –

their names are all but forgotten today and their works attract little attention in the Lower Floor galleries. From the moment of the Gallery's foundation in 1824, it was assumed that its attentions should be focussed on earlier art, particularly the Italian masters of the sixteenth and seventeenth centuries. Nothing prohibited the acquisition of contemporary art. A large collection of modern British painting was in fact soon built up as a result of the Vernon Gift of 1847 and the Turner Bequest of 1856. But the modern foreign schools were entirely ignored as unworthy of consideration. Although he had spent much time in Paris in 1814 and 1815, Sir Charles Eastlake, the Gallery's first Director and a painter himself, had little more than contempt for French art: 'A crying defect in all French painters,' he wrote, 'though perhaps not so much their fault as their country's, is that *gôut libre* which is such a terrible abuse of the art.' When he and Lady Eastlake visited the Salon of 1861 they concluded, 'French Art is now of a class in which neither the most indulgent nor the most enlightened age can see merit.'

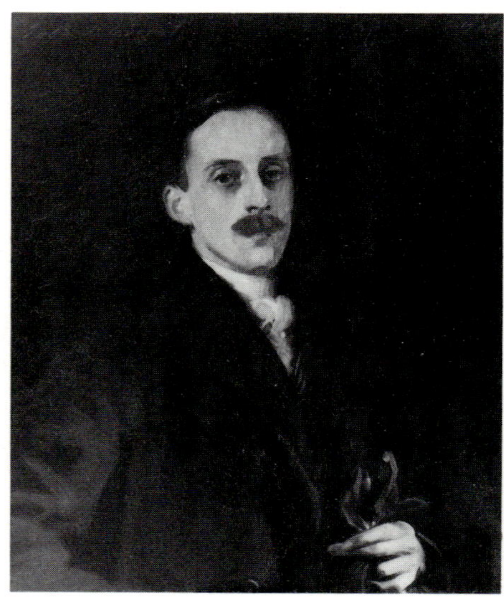

Portrait of Sir Hugh Lane *by J. S. Sargent. 1906. Dublin, The Hugh Lane Municipal Gallery of Modern Art.*

Eastlake's prejudices were broadly inherited by his immediate successors at the National Gallery. Consequently at a time when major works by living artists could have been acquired for modest sums in comparison with those that the Gallery spent on Old Master paintings, the contemporary field was ignored. A great Collection of Italian, Dutch, Flemish, and *earlier* French painting was constructed, for which the country owes an enormous debt of gratitude. Thanks to the efforts of Eastlake, and his successors Boxall and Burton, we can boast an Italian Collection second to none outside Italy. But the neglect of the nineteenth century has been impossible entirely to repair. By the time the Gallery became aware of its needs in this field the great masterpieces had already been snapped up by American, German and French museums, or if they appeared on the market were to be hotly contested by wealthy collectors.

Nevertheless, the nineteenth-century Collection is not meagre, as the contents of this book show. Due to some energetic, if belated, activity and the generosity of certain benefactors, a holding of major paintings was established by 1930 which still, in spite of more recent purchases, represents the nucleus of the nineteenth-century Collection.

The earliest substantial group of such paintings to enter the Gallery formed part of the Salting Bequest of 1910. But while George Salting had chosen Dutch and Italian pictures with such discrimination, his taste in nineteenth-century works was for the period conservative. Of these the majority were of the Barbizon school, including paintings by Théodore Rousseau, Diaz and Daubigny, and no fewer than seven by Corot. Also among Salting's pictures were two outstanding oil sketches by Constable.

One of the earliest collectors of 'modern' French painting in this country was Sir Hugh Lane, whose initial ambition was to present

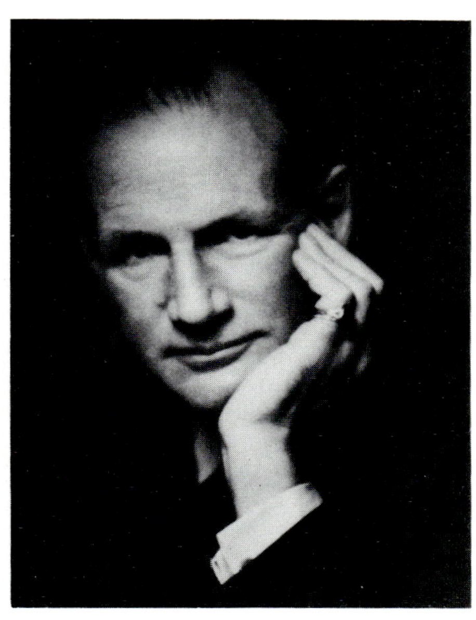

Photograph of Samuel Courtauld. Courtaulds plc.

his pictures to the city of Dublin. But when Dublin showed unwillingness to erect a gallery to house them, Lane decided to bequeath them to London. He started to buy Impressionist pictures in 1905, when Durand-Ruel brought an exhibition to London which was to prove a turning point at last for British taste. Lane purchased Manet's *Music in the Tuileries Gardens* (Plate No. 17) as well as his *Portrait of Eva Gonzalès*, Renoir's *Umbrellas* (Plate No. 30), Pissarro's *View from Louveciennes* (Plate No. 20) and a landscape by Monet. Finally the collection he bequeathed included thirty-nine paintings, among them works by Corot, Courbet, Daubigny, Daumier, Berthe Morisot and Vuillard. Unfortunately British resistance to French art sullied even Lane's generous gift. In 1913 the Trustees of the National Gallery accepted an offer of the paintings on loan, but while Lane was absent in America they decided to hang only fifteen of the pictures, considering that the remainder, including *The Umbrellas*, Daumier's *Don Quixote and Sancho Panza*, and Monet's *Vétheuil*, were unfit for exhibition. Lane objected to the Trustees' high-handed and incompetent behaviour and after his death in the Lusitania disaster of 1915 an unwitnessed codicil to his will was discovered leaving the paintings to Dublin. Consequently while the collection is legally the property of the National Gallery, a large part of it is on long-term loan to The Hugh Lane Municipal Gallery of Modern Art in Dublin.

The Lane collection was eventually put on show in 1917 in the new modern foreign galleries which had been added to the Tate Gallery (then a part of the National Gallery) through the generosity of Sir Joseph Duveen. In 1916 the Trustees had accepted a Degas pastel as a gift from Duveen and in 1918 – at the instigation of Roger Fry and Maynard Keynes – Sir Charles Holmes, Director of the National Gallery, was authorized to bid at the Degas sale. He returned from Paris with a group of major additions to the Collection, including the fragments of Manet's *Execution of Maximilian* (Plate No. 18), Delacroix's early portrait of *Baron Schwiter* (Plate No. 3), a *Flower piece* by Gauguin (Plate No. 38), four paintings by Ingres (Plate No. 7) and a number of drawings now at the British Museum. In terms of taste the purchase was nevertheless within acceptable bounds. No attempt was made to buy any of Degas' fine collection of Cézannes.

The Lane Bequest and the Degas sale, however, were but prologues to the most sensational spate of purchasing which in less than a decade secured over twenty major works by Manet, Renoir, Degas, Monet, Pissarro, Cézanne, Seurat, Van Gogh and Toulouse-Lautrec for the Collection. Samuel Courtauld, an industrialist whose love of Impressionist and Post-Impressionist art had developed during the early decades of the century into an ambition to convert his countrymen to these yet neglected painters, built the finest private collection of French painting this country has known, the greater part of which he gave to the University of

London and can today be seen at the Courtauld Institute Galleries. He also magnificently endowed the National Collections with a gift in 1923 of £50,000 for the purchase of Impressionist and Post-Impressionist paintings. Administered by a committee of five, including Courtauld himself and the Directors of the National and Tate Galleries, the Courtauld Fund was thus set up and within two years acquired, among other great paintings, three outstanding Van Goghs – *A Cornfield with Cypresses* (Plate No. 37), the *Sunflowers* (Plate No. 35) and *The Chair and the Pipe* (Plate No. 36), and Seurat's masterpiece, the monumental *Bathers, Asnières* (Plate No. 31). The purchases made by the Fund established, at a date when top quality works of this kind were becoming increasingly difficult to acquire, the basis of a great collection of nineteenth-century foreign painting. Without Courtauld's far-sighted generosity, some of the artists whose works appear in this book might yet be unrepresented in the National Gallery.

Of the fifty pictures illustrated here, seven formed part of the Lane Bequest, five were acquired at the Degas sale, and twelve were purchased by the Courtauld Fund. Almost a third, however, have been acquired in the last twenty years, an indication of how, in recompense for past neglect and in recognition of the master status of the great painters of the nineteenth century, the Gallery has concentrated much of its resources in recent years on developing this part of the Collection. Some of the works acquired are by artists not previously represented, whose paintings are still comparatively little known in England, for example 'Le Douanier' Rousseau (Plate No. 40), Gustave Moreau (Plate No. 39), and Odilon Redon (Plate No. 46). Important late paintings by Monet and Renoir have been purchased (Plates Nos. 49 & 50) as well as prime examples from the 1870s. *The Seine at Asnières* by Renoir (Plate No. 29) and Monet's *Gare Saint-Lazare* (Plate No. 24) also serve to perpetuate the connection with Samuel Courtauld since they were both once part of his private collection. Furthermore the generous bequest by Mrs Walzer in 1979 of *Bathers at La Grenouillère* (Plate No. 19) by Monet has contribued to the Collection one of the key works of early Impressionism.

The earlier period has also been cultivated, with the purchase in 1976 of a characteristic late religious painting by Delacroix to add to the small but very fine group of works by the artist, and, in 1978, by the purchase of Millet's *The Winnower* (Plate No. 10) at auction in New York. Until then the Gallery possessed only one painting by the artist – a small, early pastoral scene in his so-called *manière fleurie*. *The Winnower* is by contrast a Realist work of major importance which was to have a lasting influence on French painting.

Through the combined efforts of benefactors and Gallery staff and Trustees a substantial and impressive nineteenth-century French collection has now been built up. Yet in these efforts is the

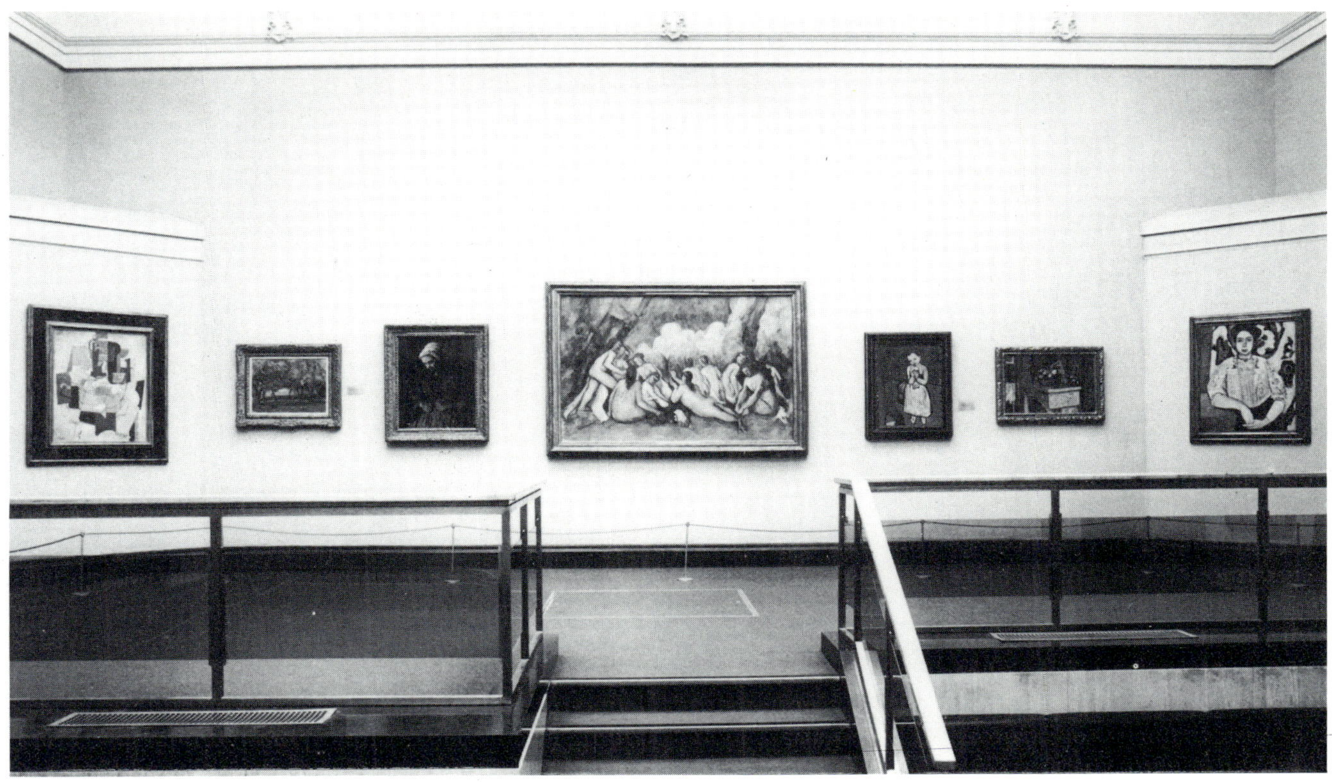

Photograph of part of Room 45, including paintings by Cézanne, Vuillard, Picasso and Matisse.

Gallery in danger again of neglecting what is closest at hand, the production of living artists? This danger has been averted, since when it was established as an independent National Museum in 1954, the Tate Gallery was given responsibility for the Modern Foreign Collection as well as the British Collection. Nevertheless, as painters achieve classic status and cease to be truly 'modern' it behoves the National Gallery to try to display their works at Trafalgar Square, alongside the paintings of their predecessors whose innovations they themselves were to take up and develop along new lines. Thus in Room 45, a Cubist still-life of 1914 by Picasso (Plate No. 48) purchased in 1979 hangs beside the work of Cézanne, and an early portrait by Matisse (Plate No. 47), purchased in the same year, beside paintings by Vuillard and Van Gogh, demonstrating the tangible links between French nineteenth-century painting and the art of our own century.

PLATE 1

Jean-Louis-André-Théodore Géricault, 1791–1824

A Horse frightened by Lightning (No. 4927)

Canvas, 49 × 60 cm.
Purchased 1938

Géricault's brief life was consumed by strong passions – passionate love affairs, adulation of heroes, Rubens and Michelangelo above all, and a love of horses. His death resulted from a fall from a horse. He hurt his spine, neglected the injury, contracted an abscess, and after awful suffering died at the age of only thirty-three.

The drama of Géricault's life was set against turbulent events. He was born shortly after the Revolution and as a youth witnessed Napoleon's great campaigns of conquest, culminating in 1815 in his final defeat and exile. No wonder that horses and soldiers had such an irresistible appeal for this young man of emotional character. He chose at the age of seventeen to train in the studio of Carle Vernet, a fashionable horse painter, and formed a life-long friendship with Vernet's son, Horace. After two years he decided to enter the studio of Guérin, a pupil of David, who was nevertheless tolerant of his gifted pupil's immoderate admiration of Rubens. The vigorous method of handling he adopted, with heavy impasto, earned him the nickname among his fellow pupils of '*le cuisinier de Rubens*'.

He participated at the Salon for the first time in 1812, when he exhibited a huge canvas representing an *Officer of the Imperial Guard* which won him a gold medal. The baroque movement of the rearing horse and twisting rider stem from Rubens, but his immediate model for the heroic image of a soldier galloping into battle was Baron Gros, who had painted enormous canvases in a vigorous painterly style commemorating Napoleon's campaigns.

This small painting of a horse is close in date to the *Officer of the Imperial Guard*, and shows on a much smaller scale the same excitable temperament at work, and the same energetic handling, with the creamy paint rapidly brushed on. As a keen horseman Géricault had all the expert knowledge of the specialist horse-painter, but even in modest pictures of this kind he far exceeds the scope of a Carle Vernet, and imbues the creature with a restless nervous energy. The horse is electrified by fear, as it stands sleek and poised for movement. Creamy highlights flicker along the contours of its tautened neck, like the lightning that zig-zags across the sky, illuminating the fringes of a storm cloud.

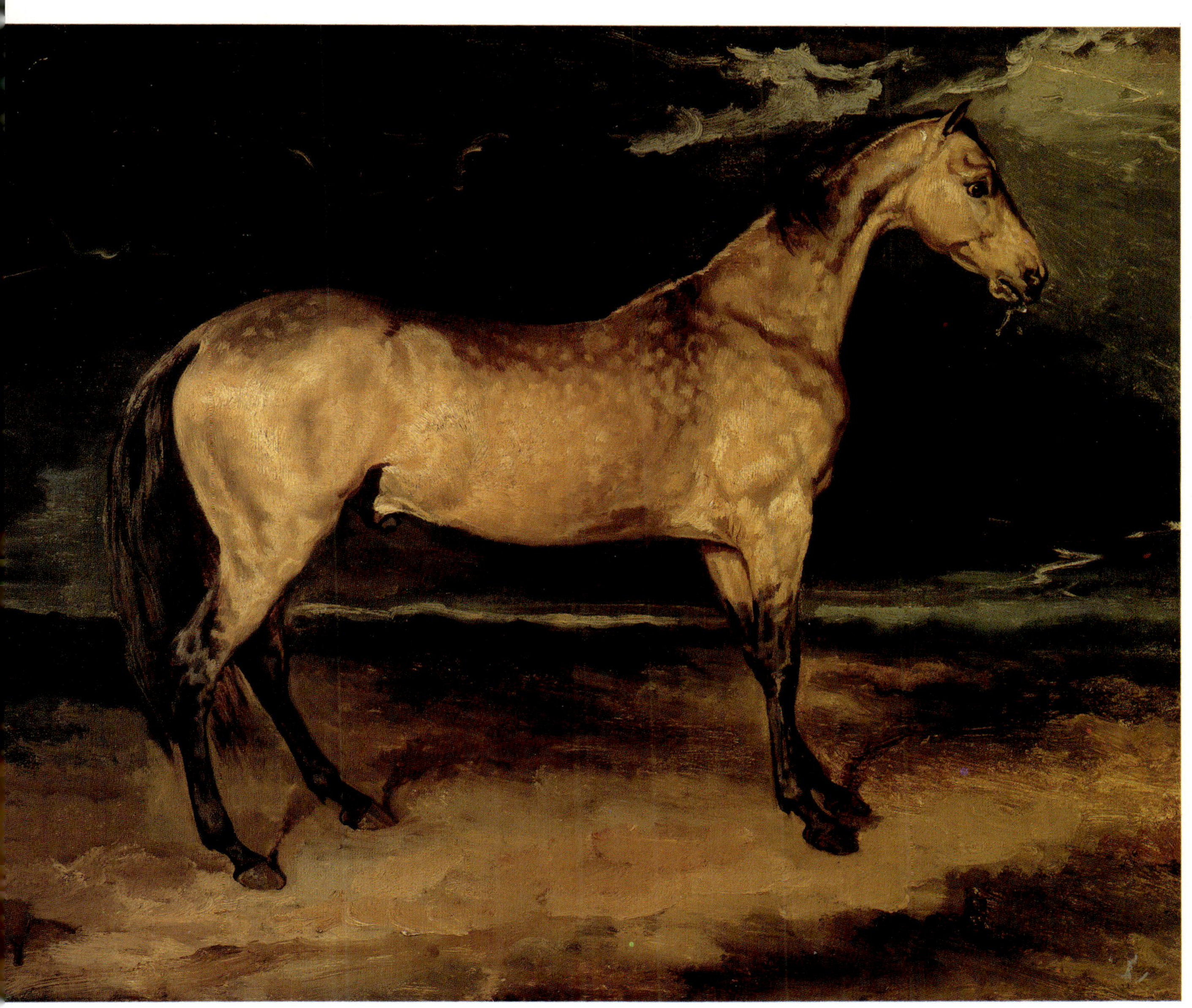

PLATE 2

Emile-Jean-Horace Vernet, 1789–1863

The Battle of Hanau (1813) (No. 2966)

Signed: Horace Vernet 1824

Canvas, 174 × 290 cm.

Bequeathed by Sir John Murray Scott 1914

Horace Vernet was one of the most important nineteenth-century exponents of battle painting, a genre which in the hands of his successors, Meissonier and Detaille, was to degenerate in less heroic times into mere picturesque story-telling. Born in the year of the Revolution, the son and grandson of painters, Horace Vernet had his career mapped out for him. As a youth under the Empire, he made drawings of soldiers; and at the Salon of 1812 he made his debut with *The Taking of a Fortress.* He helped to defend Paris against enemy troops, and for his part was awarded the *Légion d'Honneur* by Napoleon. Vernet's success continued under successive regimes. In 1826 he was elected to the Institut and from 1828 until 1833 was Director of the French Academy in Rome. He served as official painter to Louis-Philippe and Napoleon III and died in 1863 one of the most famous and fêted painters in Europe.

This huge battle painting is one of four which Vernet painted for the Duc d'Orléans, the future King Louis-Philippe. The others, *The Battle of Jemappes* painted in 1821, *The Battle of Montmirail* in 1822, and *The Battle of Valmy* in 1826 are also in the National Gallery, all four pictures having been bequeathed to the Gallery by Sir John Murray Scott, to whom they passed by descent from Lord Hertford who bought them at the Louis-Philippe sale in 1851. They had been damaged by fire in 1848 but were restored by Vernet himself.

Although painted during the reactionary period of the Restoration (and the *Battle of Jemappes* was rejected by the Salon of 1822 on account of its anti-royalist sentiment) the four paintings represent French victories of the previous era: the battles of Valmy and Jemappes of 1792 were landmarks in the French Revolutionary Wars, Hanau (1813) and Montmirail (1814), late successes of the Napoleonic campaigns. The Duc d'Orléans had served in these campaigns and Vernet's paintings record his personal memories as well as the historical circumstances. In each painting the foreground is devoted to detailed incident. Recognizable individuals are portrayed, commanding events, engaged in combat, or expiring heroically on the field. In the distance the lines of troops are shown disposed across the panorama of the battlefield.

In the autumn of 1813, the Campaign of Leipzig (the Battle of the Nations) forced Napoleon to retire west of the Rhine. In the course of this retreat, on 13 October 1813, the French heavily defeated a force of Germans under Wrede at Hanau, near Frankfurt. In Vernet's painting the French have overwhelmed a cannon position. A group of officers stand to the left, a company of grenadiers advance through the woods on the right, passing a bewildered soldier who walks away from the battle. In the centre a group are engaged in heroic combat, while in the plain beyond the cavalry are shown charging. Each incident is depicted in painstaking detail, and the entire canvas is put together with wholehearted enthusiasm and consummate skill.

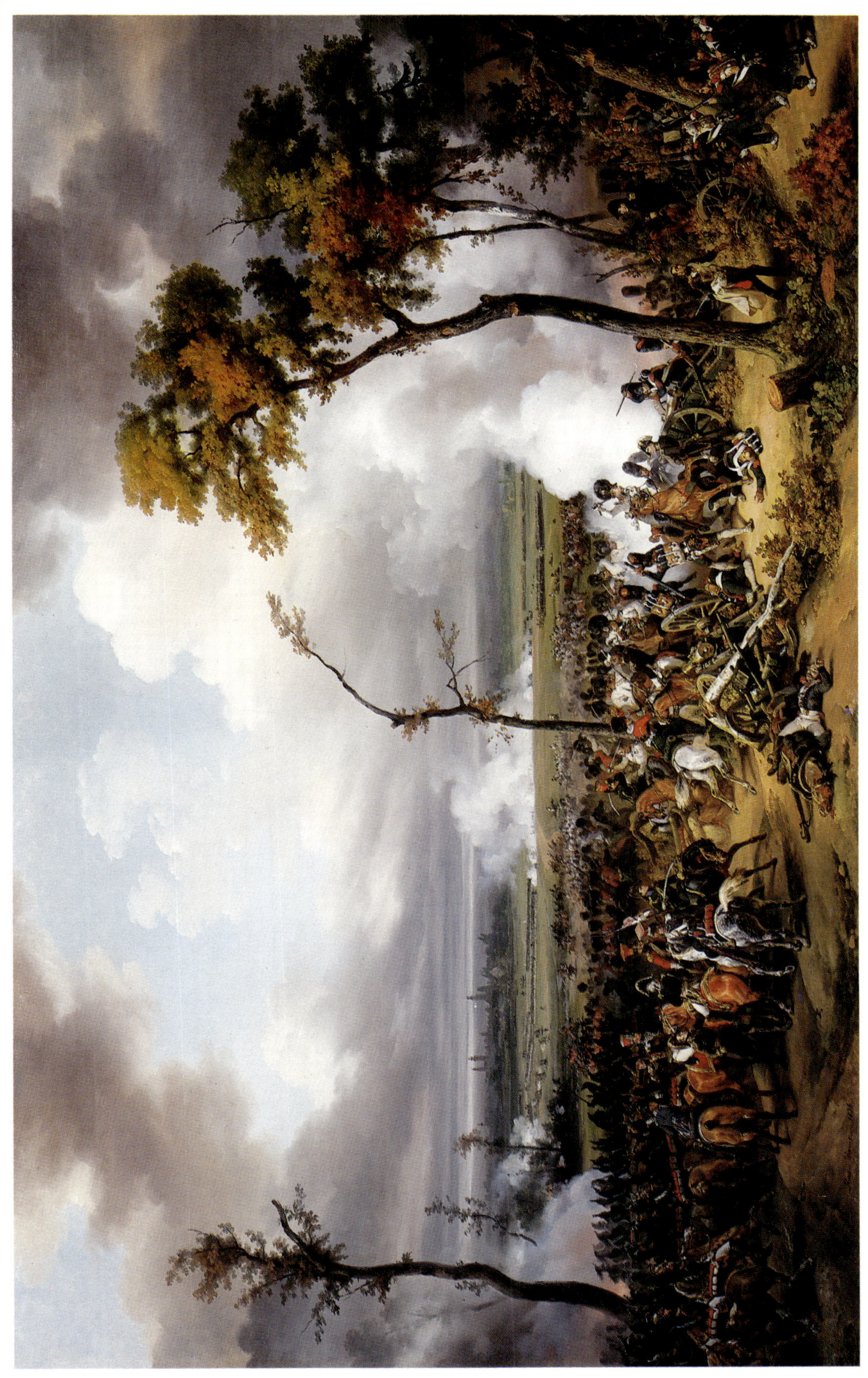

PLATE 3

Ferdinand-Victor-Eugène Delacroix, 1798–1863

Baron Schwiter (No. 3286)

Signed: Euge Delacroix
Canvas, 218 × 143 cm.
Purchased 1918

This impressive portrait was begun soon after a long visit that Delacroix made to England in 1825, and reveals in its conception and its handling the deep influence English painting had upon the young French artist.

Even before his visit Delacroix had developed a taste for things English, for Shakespeare and Byron, for the technique of watercolour and for the caricatures of Rowlandson and Gillray. In London, in spite of the awful weather, he was able to indulge his taste for English drama, and make the acquaintance of a number of eminent painters, including William Etty, Sir David Wilkie, John Constable and Sir Thomas Lawrence, in Delacroix's words: 'the flower of politeness and truly the painter of great men'.

The virtuoso, almost Venetian handling of these painters was a revelation to Delacroix, brought up in the school of David, and left a permanent mark on his style. In the portrait of Baron Louis-Auguste Schwiter (1805–89), a painter of portraits and landscapes who exhibited at the Salon from 1831 until 1859, and a personal friend of Delacroix, the enthusiasm for British painting can be felt in the sonorous shadows, the Van Dyckian black of the sitter's outfit, the sombre landscape and the liquid highlights that flicker across the surface.

According to one early biographer, part of the landscape was painted by Paul Huet, a fellow-student of Delacroix at the studio of Guérin, and the leading landscapist of the Romantic school in France. But in spite of their close contacts, it seems unlikely that Delacroix would have needed assistance. The treatment of the various parts of the picture is entirely consistent and well within his capabilities. For the distant landscape with its lush greens and pools of light he has looked at Constable, while the concept of a single subject posed on a terrace and the execution of the figure owe more to Lawrence. It was from him that Delacroix learned the decorative and sensuous possibilities of creamy paint, effortlessly applied: in the knot of a high-necked stock, in the sheen of a pair of black pumps, or in the glaze of an earthenware pot. Delacroix did experience some difficulty with this life-size portrait. It was rejected by the Salon of 1827 and not finally completed until 1830; yet in the sinuous folds of the black frock coat, the writhing fronds of foliage, and even in the elegant signature, it is already evident how Delacroix was able to imbue animate and inanimate form alike with an insistent nervous energy.

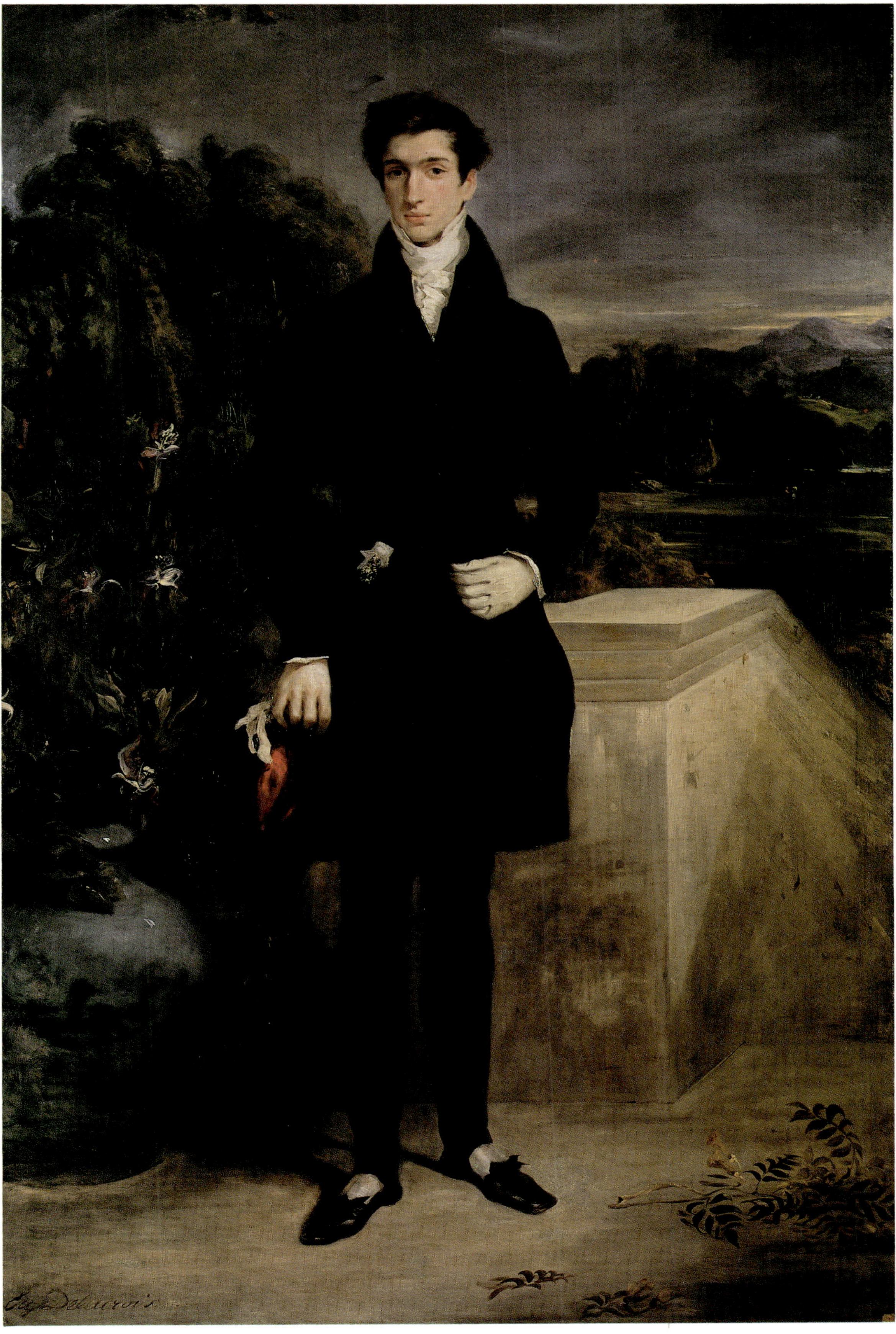

PLATE 4

Paul Delaroche, 1795–1856

The Execution of Lady Jane Grey (No. 1909)

Signed: Paul DelaRoche 1833
Canvas, 246 × 297 cm.
Bequeathed 1902

Paul Delaroche is scarcely remembered today, but during the 1830s and 40s his pictures enjoyed an enormous international vogue. While high-brow art critics and painters of pretension were divided in their allegiance between Ingres, the master of line, and Delacroix, the champion of colour, Delaroche steered a middle course and adopted a sufficiently naturalistic style to win the support of the vast majority of visitors to the Paris Salon exhibitions. He chose violent and emotionally appealing subjects, mostly death-scenes, and painted them in a direct, anecdotal manner. Following the success of Walter Scott's novels he encouraged and exploited current Anglomania and the fashion for subjects from sixteenth- and seventeenth-century history, making the most of the picturesque possibilities of period costume and architecture. He took great pains to get his story right; the *livret* of the 1834 Salon specifies that the source for *The Execution of Lady Jane Grey* was a Protestant Martyrology of 1588. The painting depicts the moment of execution of the grand-daughter of Henry VII who reigned for nine brief days in 1553 after the death of Edward VI, until her capture and imprisonment by the supporters of Mary I. She was beheaded at the Tower of London on 12 February 1554.

The Execution of Lady Jane Grey created a sensation at the Salon of 1834 and still today wins the admiration of those who like a story with a sad ending. The pretty, blind-folded girl, brought to her death by the evil scheming of the ugly Queen Mary, pathetically reaches forward to feel her way to the block. How winning she is, kneeling in her white satin dress on a velvet cushion, her golden tresses falling across her tragically bared neck! The kindly Lieutenant of the Tower guides her arms, while the stern executioner looks on and the ladies-in-waiting collapse in convulsions of grief against the chill stone column. Thus with ingenious artistry the final tableau is set; the curtain is about to fall amid the thunder of applause. As the critic Gautier remarked shortly after the artist's death, 'I can't help feeling that Paul Delaroche would have had an even greater success in the theatre. It was there that his true talent lay. What skill and artistry of staging! And also, frankly, what mastery of lighting all those grisly deaths and decapitations!'

Delaroche's painting was bequeathed to the Gallery in 1902, but, while at the Tate, suffered in the Thames flood of 1928 and was thought destroyed. Only in 1973 was it found that the damage was merely superficial and the picture was returned to the National Gallery, restored, and put on exhibition again for the first time in over fifty years.

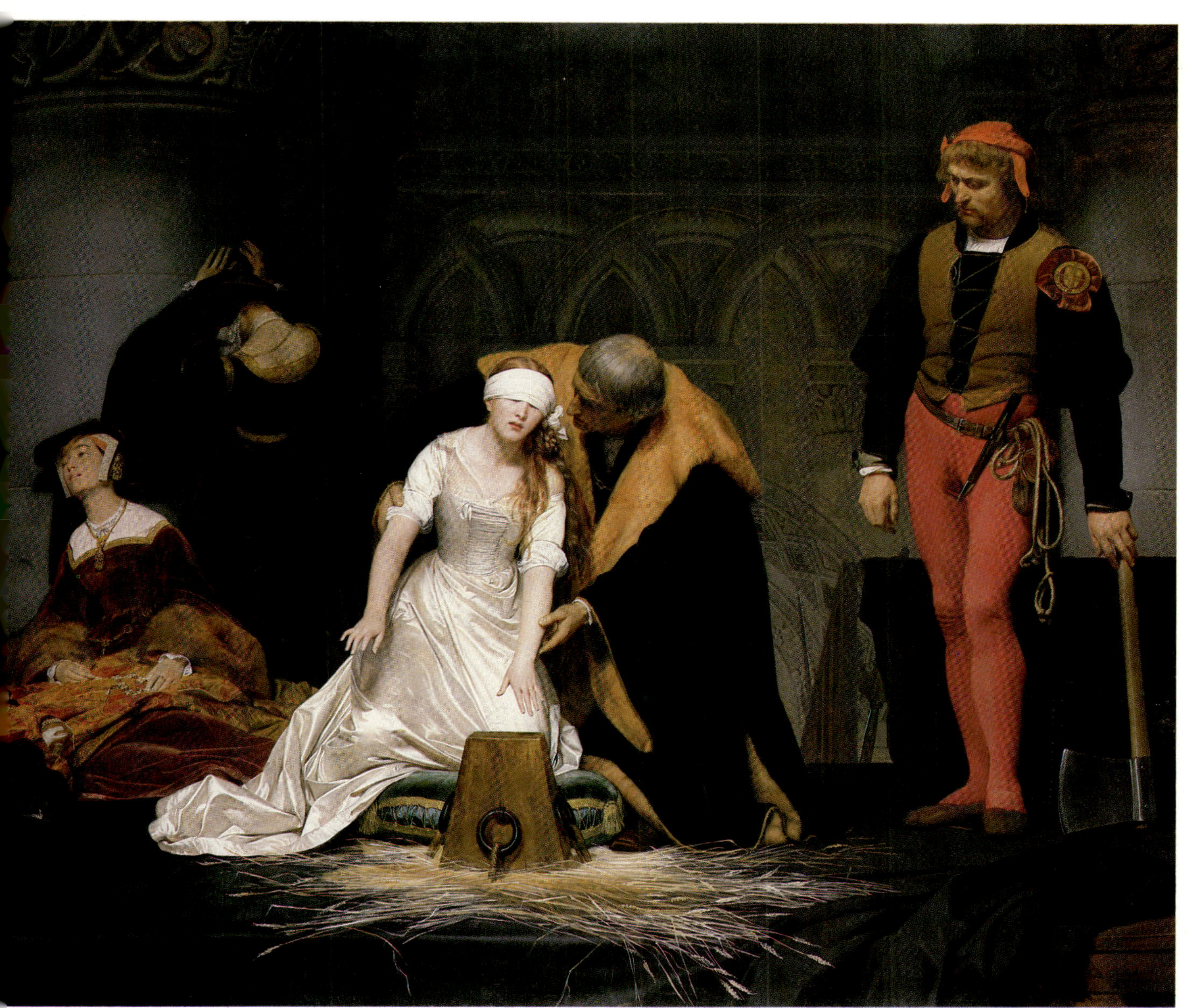

PLATE 5

Jean-Baptiste-Camille Corot, 1796–1875

The Roman Campagna, with the Claudian Aqueduct (No. 3285)

Signed: COROT
Paper on canvas, 21.6 × 33 cm.
Purchased 1918

As was the custom with painters in France early in the nineteenth century, Corot travelled to Rome for a prolonged stay between 1826 and 1828 to complete his training. His former teachers, Achille Michallon and Victor Bertin were specialists in the genre of classical landscape and had both previously worked in Rome and the surrounding countryside. There they sketched the ruins and classical statuary with which they filled the landscapes that they subsequently composed in the studio. And they studied the works of the great landscapists of the seventeenth century, Claude, Poussin and Gaspard Dughet, who had worked in the Campagna before them and whose example they followed.

Corot, however, had little interest in studying the Old Masters or the ruins of Rome, and preferred to devote all his time to painting in the open. He still frequented the popular sites. This tiny sketch was painted from near the Via Appia Nuova and shows in the distance the long low Papal Aqueduct, the Acqua Felice, and on each side the ruins of the arched Claudian Aqueduct, with the Alban Hills beyond. But these historic edifices are no more than incidental details in the landscape, serving as tonal accents along the horizon. The real interest of the sketch lies in the way Corot has established the huge expanse of plain and the majestic cloudscape above with the most economical of means. The thin dry paint scarcely covers the paper; the foreground bushes and shadows are laid in with the briefest scribble. Yet the tonal relationships are sure, and succeed in conveying a vivid impression of light and air.

When Corot painted his sketch of the Roman Campagna, no-one would have considered that it had any value except as a preparatory study for a studio composition. But during an uneventful career of over fifty years, Corot calmly persisted with his *plein-air* sketches, encouraging other painters to do likewise, and setting an example which was to be taken up and explored in the second half of the century by the Impressionists.

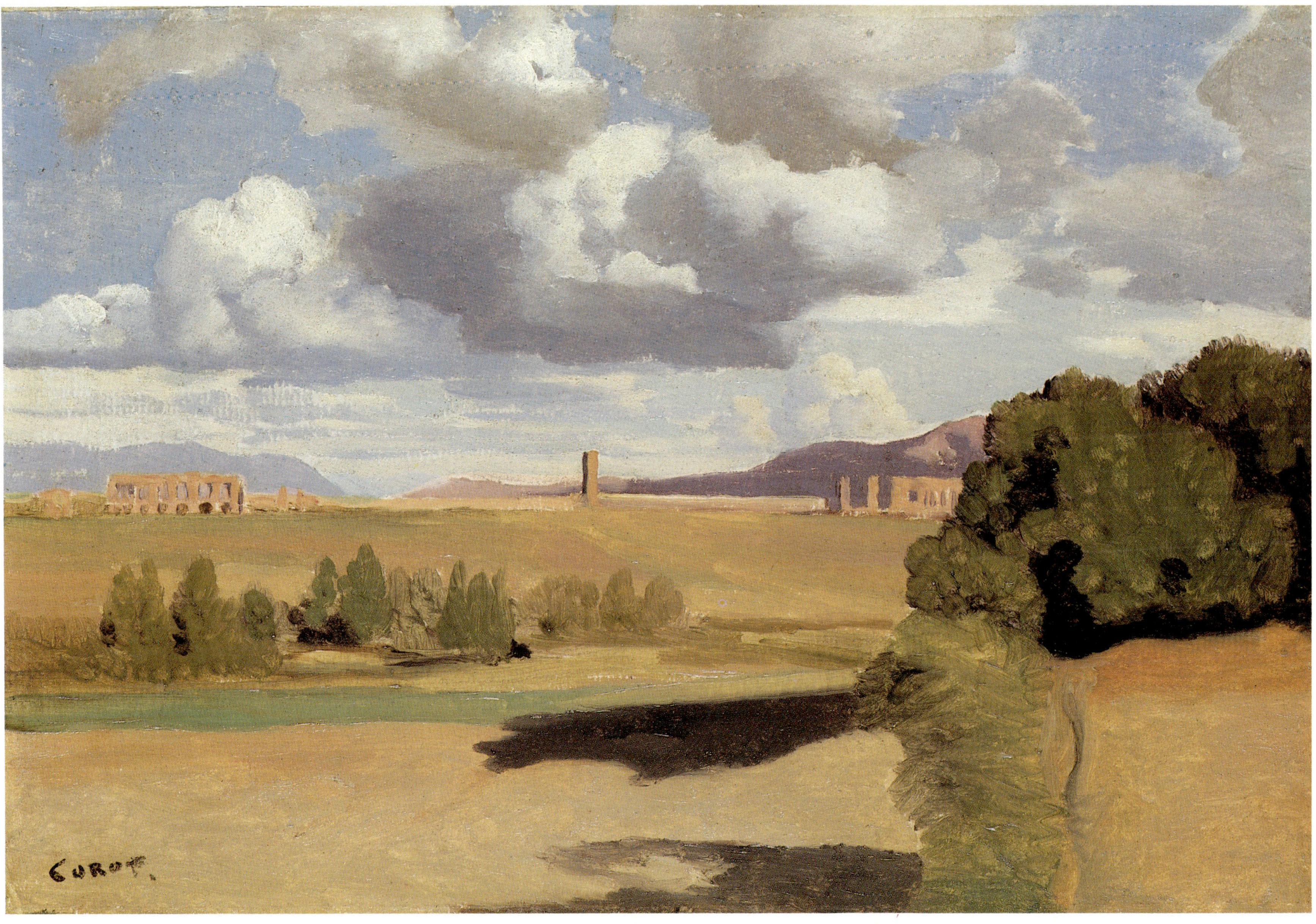
COROT.

PLATE 6

Jean-Baptiste-Camille Corot, 1796–1875

Avignon from the West (No. 3237)

Signed: COROT
Canvas, 33.7 × 73 cm.
Lane Bequest 1917

Probably painted when Corot visited Avignon in July 1836, this picture dates from the great decade of the Romantic movement. It is only two years later than Delaroche's melodramatic *Execution of Lady Jane Grey* which invites us to delight in hysterical emotion, historical trappings and a pathetic death. Another artist would have made much more of the historic site of Avignon, the famous medieval city dominated by its colossal Palace of the Popes, dotted with churches, and proudly boasting the ruined Pont Saint-Bénézet, as celebrated in the popular song (and just visible in Corot's painting to the left of the main mass of the town). But Corot's painting does not read as a tourist's itinerary. Instead the city reclines along the banks of the Rhône, a straggling line of pale stone baking in the hot afternoon sun, one building scarcely distinguishable from another, mute and placid.

Corot had little interest in the excesses of the Romantics or in the idealized allegories of Ingres and the Classicists. He would submit landscapes representing *The Flight into Egypt* or *Hagar and the Angel* for exhibition at the Salon, but the bulk of his work consisted of modest-sized oil sketches of real locations, painted for the most part in the open.

Landscapes such as this demonstrate the clarity and immediacy of his response to nature. He organizes the varied forms of hills, trees and massed buildings into a balanced structure, simplifying and clarifying detail to achieve a remarkable truth to nature. He does likewise with colour, finely modulating each tone, so that the warm greens and earth colours of the foreground imperceptibly recede into the cool blues of the mountains, to create an overall harmony which is richly suggestive of a warm afternoon in southern France.

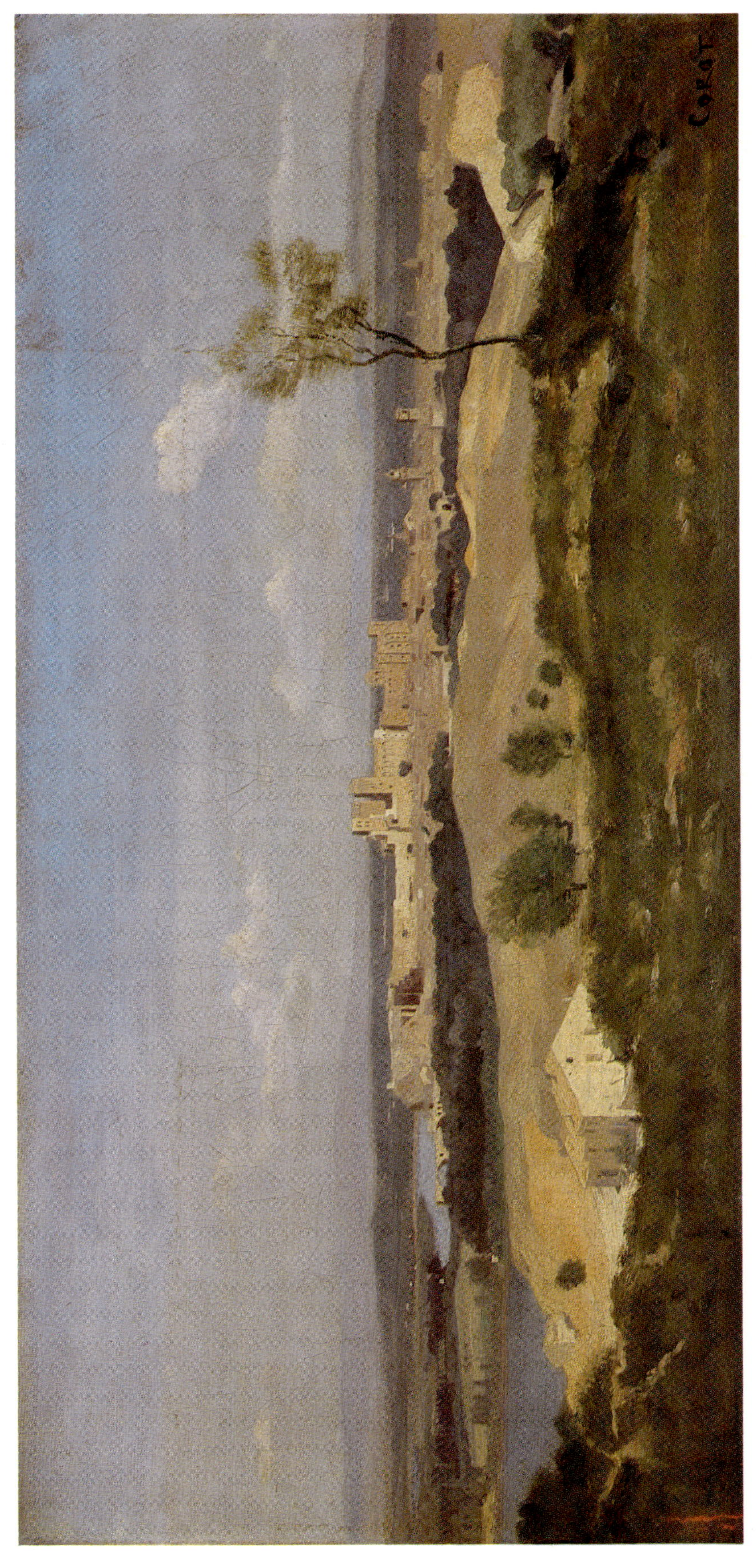

PLATE 7

Jean-Auguste-Dominique Ingres, 1780–1867

Angelica saved by Ruggiero (No. 3292)

Signed: Ingres P[it].
Canvas, 47.6 × 39.4 cm.
Purchased 1918

It is hard to believe that this little picture was painted by the leading classical painter of the nineteenth century, the man who denounced Delacroix as decadent and never tired of asserting the primacy of Raphael and Greek and Roman art. But then how entirely characteristic of Ingres is the softly contoured form of Angelica, her head thrown back at an impossible angle above an unnaturally swollen neck.

Although Ingres always preached conformity to the doctrines of classicism, he could never suppress his intensely personal sensibility which constantly led him astray from the orthodox path, like 'a Chinese or Japanese artist lost in the streets of Paris' as he was once described. When the original version of this composition (today in the Louvre) was shown at the 1819 Salon, it was greeted by scorn and incomprehension, and led one critic to ask 'does he want to lead us back to the infancy of art?' In fact Ingres designed the Louvre picture as an overdoor for the throne room at Versailles, and the subject was specified for him. It is taken from Ariosto's epic poem *Orlando Furioso*, at the moment when the hero Ruggiero, mounted on a Hippogriff (a mythological creature comprising part bird and part horse), saves the captive Angelica from a sea monster. Themes of medieval romance such as this were just enjoying a new vogue in France and marked a break from the painter's usual stock-in-trade of classical myths and histories.

Although the critics proved not to be ready for such a revolution in taste, Ingres was pleased enough with his performance to repeat it with variations more than once. This upright version is not dated but was lithographed in 1839. Another similar version at Montauban bears the date 1841. In both of them Ingres has brought the distant rock and lighthouse to the centre of the picture and improved on his monster, the Orc, giving it a long tail which coils about Angelica's feet.

The subject no doubt appealed to Ingres because it permitted him to indulge in the most bizarre and, for a pupil of David, illicit effects. The drama of Angelica's rescue unfolds against a fantastic night-scene; a flickering beacon casts an eerie gleam on the sea, and an unnatural radiance illumines the figures. The action is frozen, as though in a medieval illustration, allowing us the time to appreciate the loving detail with which Ingres had depicted the beautiful plumage of the Hippogriff, the elaborately chased armour of his hero, and the bejewelled hair of the heroine. Ingres invites us to savour with him the gamut of strange textures with which the little canvas is stuffed – metal, feather, claw, scale, hair, rock, flesh – and above all to relish the opposition between Ruggiero, who is all things hard and sharp, and the limp, boneless Angelica. One of Ingres' most famous creations, she has won many admirers, including the painters Tissot, Whistler, Seurat and Degas, each of whom copied her extraordinary form.

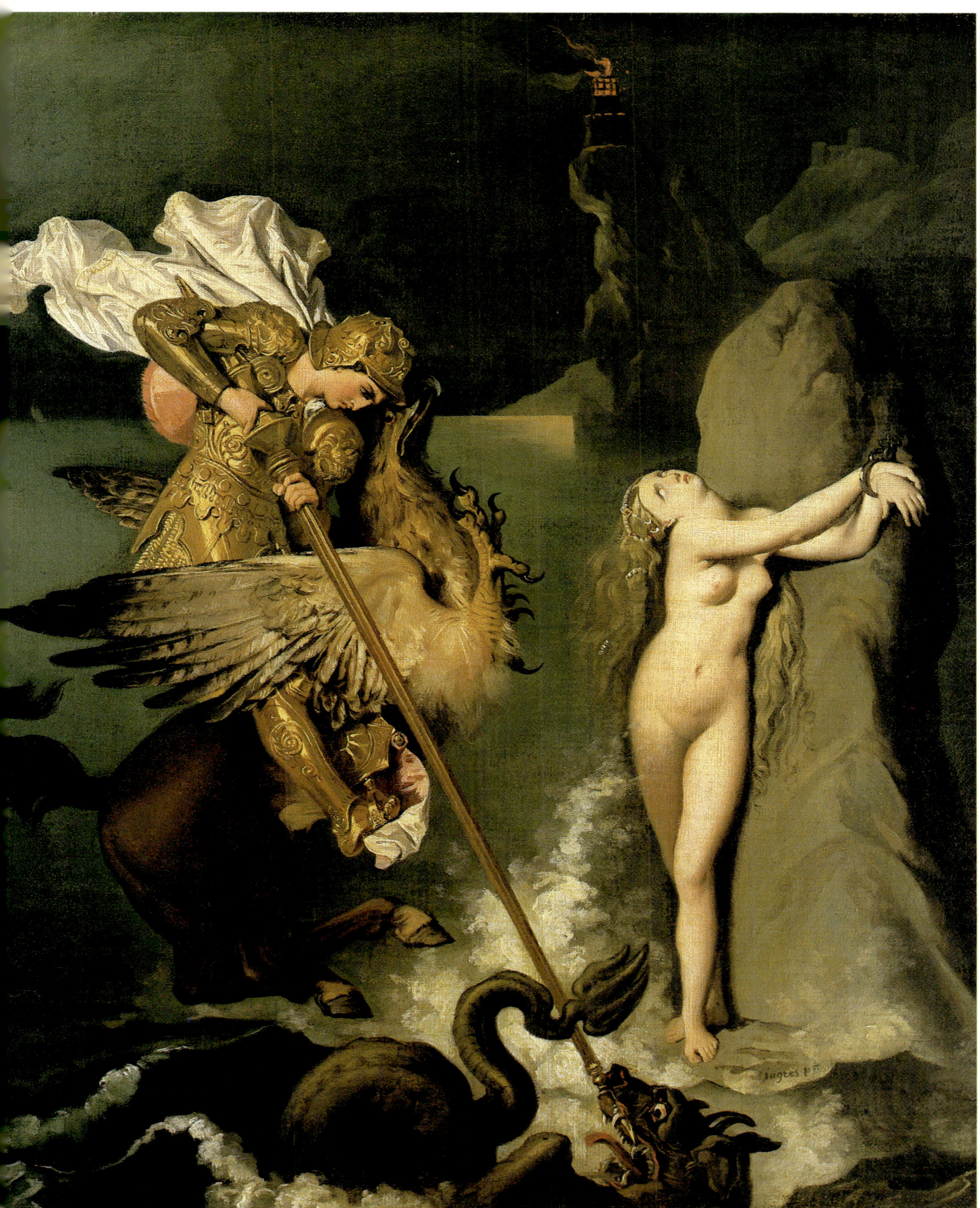

PLATE 8

Jean-Auguste-Dominique Ingres, 1780–1867

Madame Moitessier seated (No. 4821)

Inscribed: Me INÈS MOITESSIER/NÉE DE FOUCAULD
Signed: J. Ingres 1856/AET LXXVI
Canvas, 120 × 92 cm.
Purchased 1936

When the critic Gautier saw this late portrait in Ingres' studio in 1847, he wrote of it, 'never has beauty of a type more regal, more splendid, more superb and more Juno-like delivered up its proud lines to the trembling pencil of an artist'. The young Madame Moitessier so appealed to Ingres that he worked on her portrait over twelve years, eventually completing it in 1856 when he was seventy-six – as he has proudly recorded in the inscription on the frame of the mirror. She represented for him an ideal of classical beauty, ample, impassive, flawless and goddess-like. The distinctive pose with hand raised to cheek he borrowed from a Roman wall-painting, a personification of Arcadia, which he may have seen in Naples in 1814, and the classical allusion is reinforced by the sphinx-like profile in the mirror.

But the polished perfection of the finished portrait was not easily achieved. It cost the artist years of suffering. Always reluctant to undertake portraits when he believed, mistakenly, that his reputation depended upon large historical compositions, Ingres at first refused to paint the twenty-three-year-old Inès Moitessier when asked by her husband, a wealthy banker, in 1844. But when he met her shortly after, he consented, captivated by her beauty.

For five years Ingres worked on the canvas, at one stage including the sitter's young daughter, Catherine, who proved to be 'insupportable' and was struck out, until in 1849 his wife died and, inconsolable and desperately lonely, he abandoned the picture. Eventually, in 1851, tired of waiting, Madame Moitessier urged Ingres to return to her portrait, but instead of completing the unfinished picture, he painted another portrait of her – standing, in black – which is now in the National Gallery, Washington. Ingres, however, was still not satisfied, and returned again to his original conception, working on it for yet another five years.

Concerned that his sitter should appear absolutely *à la mode*, Ingres took great pains over her costume. The dress he changed three times, finally choosing a daringly busy floral print, supported by a wide hooped crinoline, the revolutionary innovation in women's fashions of 1855. Madame Moitessier has also adopted the bare-faced look, with hair pulled off the brow *à l'Impératrice*, a style which only became fashionable in the mid-fifties. Second Empire taste asserts itself again in the rococo-revival furniture, so that for all its classical allusions the portrait is ultimately of its time. Plump and secure, Madame Moitessier is a goddess of the drawing room, and represents the triumph of bourgeois materialism and opulence.

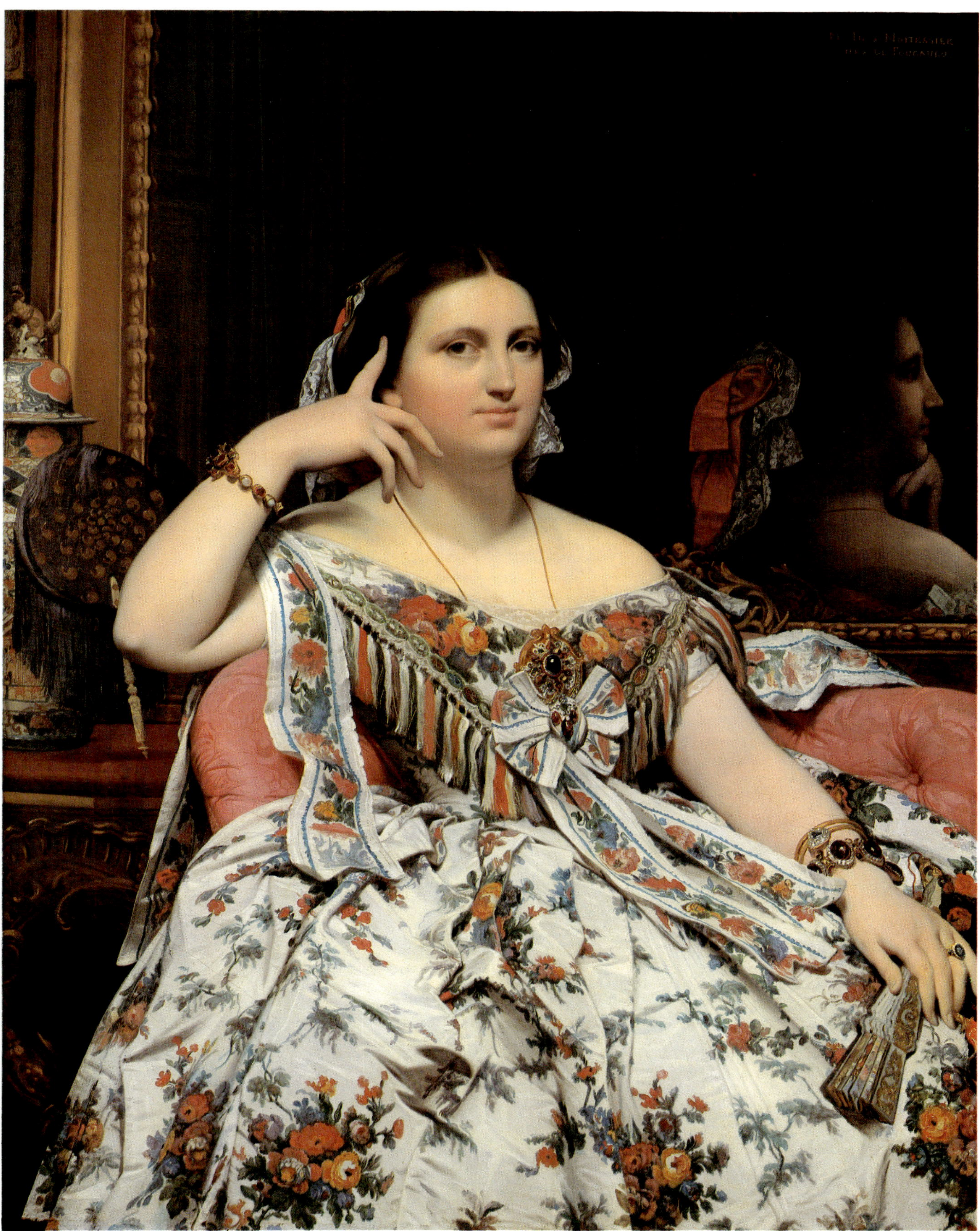

PLATE 9

Ferdinand-Victor-Eugène Delacroix, 1798–1863

Ovid among the Scythians (No. 6262)

Signed: Eug. Delacroix 1859
Canvas, 88 × 130 cm.
Purchased 1956

The theme of the Roman poet Ovid in exile had a special appeal for Delacroix. He treated it in part of his decoration of the Library of the Chambre des Députés in Paris as well as in this painting which was exhibited at the Salon of 1859. The subject represented for Delacroix the ingratitude and incomprehension that is the lot of the great artist. In AD 8 the Emperor Augustus banished Ovid to Tomi, a bleak fishing village on the coast of the Black Sea, for some unknown indiscretion, and in spite of his constant petitions the poet passed the last ten years of his life there among primitive tribes.

Although by the time he painted this picture Delacroix had completed a number of important government commissions and was popularly recognized as one of France's leading painters, he still believed that he was not properly appreciated. Only in 1857, at the seventh attempt, was he elected to the *Institut*, and after his poor reception at the 1859 Salon he decided not to exhibit there again. Living a solitary existence in Paris, with only his housekeeper as company, he believed himself to be like Ovid, an artist surrounded by uncomprehending barbarians.

In Delacroix's painting, the Scythians make tentative advances to the downcast Ovid who lies apart, with head bowed, detached, vulnerable, and as unlike them as a creature from another planet. The figures are almost lost in the wide expanse of empty landscape, and behind them, at the centre of the picture, the featureless water forms a void. The curving fall of the distant cliffs reinforces the melancholy mood and is echoed by the curve of Ovid's body turning to acknowledge the barbarians, and by the answering curve of the horse's head. With its indistinct, uncharted distances, the landscape has a disturbing, dream-like atmosphere. In his *Journal* for 1857 Delacroix recorded waking at night troubled by painful impressions: 'There will be time to despair,' he wrote, 'when these mountains which I have seen all night over my head, have crushed me for good.' The cold blue mountains in this picture weigh down on the rustic drama enacted beneath with just such a burden of sadness.

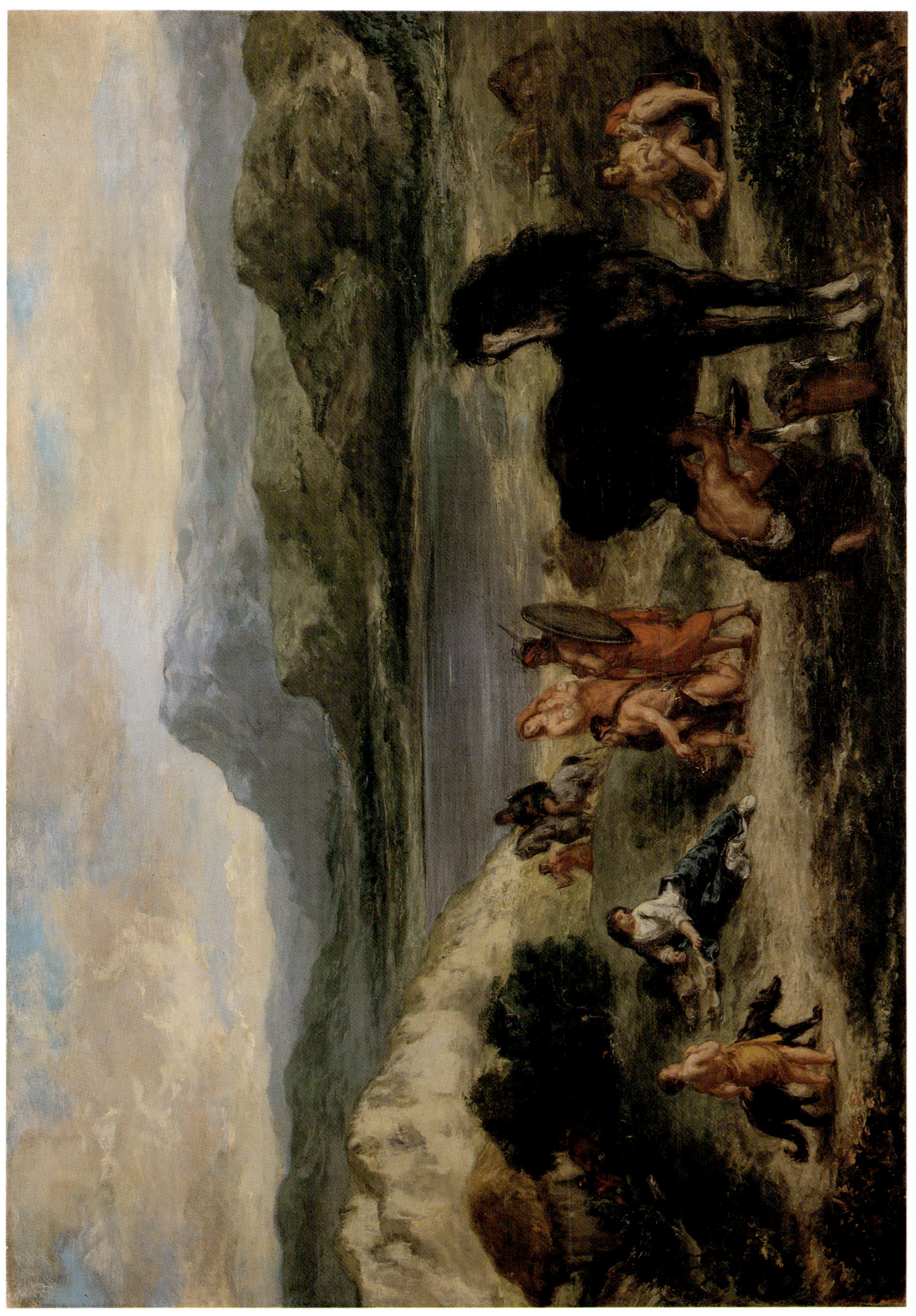

PLATE 10

Jean-François Millet, 1814–1875

The Winnower (No. 6447)

Signed: J. F. Millet
Canvas, 100 × 71 cm.
Purchased 1978

This powerful image, painted at the time of the Revolution of February 1848, was long believed to have been destroyed in the Boston fire of 1872, and the composition was known only through two smaller later variants by Millet, which differ in details of costume and are now in the Louvre. In the absence of the original version fakes were even produced but were soon exposed as such. Eventually in 1972 Millet's original painting was discovered in an attic in America, filthy but intact, and still in the original frame bearing the number under which it was registered at the Salon of 1848; and in 1978 it was bought by the Gallery at auction in New York.

The Winnower is of particular importance in the development of Millet's art. It is the first painting in which he treated a peasant subject on a large scale, anticipating *The Sower* and other monumental images of men at work of the 1850s, including Courbet's *The Stonebreakers*, which borrows the pose of *The Winnower*. In it Millet achieves a new seriousness and an emotional intensity which arises from his realization of the plight of the labourer.

Millet portrays the winnower in profile, sifting corn, against the shadowy background of the interior of a barn. The simplicity of the design throws the figure into dramatic relief, singling him out as a representative of the people. His face in shadow, he is anonymous, bowed by unremitting toil, his feet and hands swollen and red with physical effort. In keeping with the mood of the subject, the painting avoids all prettiness; it is sombrely coloured and thickly laid in. 'Nothing could be more rugged, ferocious, bristling and crude,' wrote the critic Gautier when the painting was shown at the 1848 Salon. 'M. Millet's painting has everything it takes to horrify the bourgeois.'

At the moment of the February Revolution, Millet chose this heroic image to express his Republican sentiments and his sympathy with the labouring class. The process of winnowing is itself symbolical of change, of the grain of new life being separated from the chaff, and in the red, white and blue of the winnower's costume Millet makes reference to the revolutionary flag, the Republican Tricolour. Although timeless in its human sympathy, the painting caught the mood of the time at which it was painted. At the Salon it was purchased by Ledru-Rollin, the Minister of the Interior of the new Republic, but following his fall from power it was sold and until its recent discovery disappeared from view.

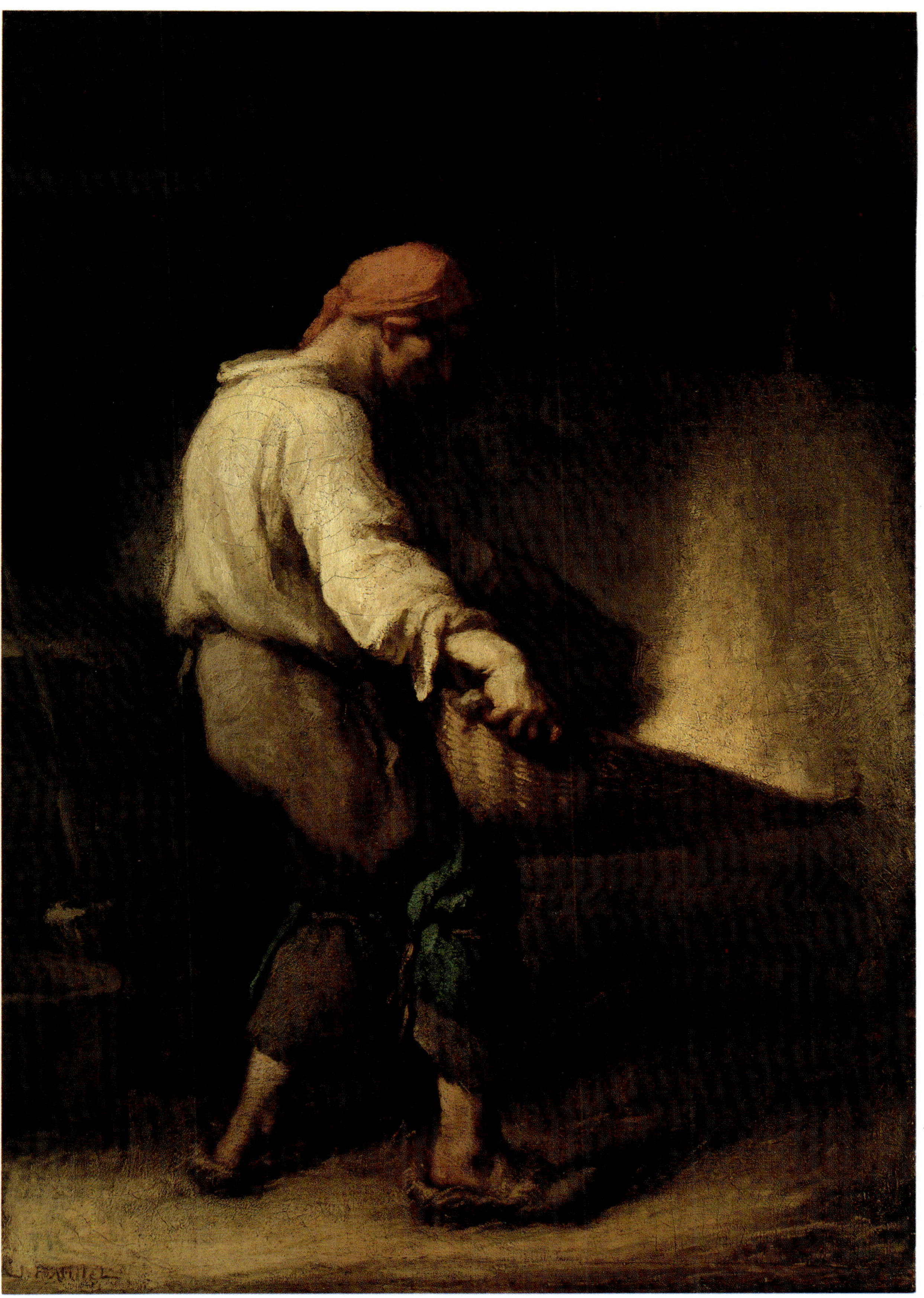

PLATE 11

Jean-Désiré-Gustave Courbet, 1819–1877

Girls on the Bank of the Seine (No. 6355)

['Les Demoiselles des Bords de la Seine']

Canvas, 96 × 130 cm.
Purchased 1964

Gustave Courbet often liked to provoke the public and the art establishment of the Second Empire, and when the large painting (now in the Musée du Petit Palais, Paris) for which this is the sketch was exhibited at the 1857 Salon, the public was suitably scandalized. 'Courbet is beating the big drum of publicity to attract the attention of an unheeding crowd,' Théophile Gautier remarked.

The sketch, although more broadly executed than the final version, corresponds to it in most respects. Only a basket of flowers at the base of the tree and certain details of jewellery are still missing. It is hard looking at it today to imagine how the image of two girls reclining beside the river on a summer's day might be considered outrageous, but these are not polite ladies. Their abandoned attitudes, heavy sensual features and shadowed eyes are a clue to their morals and their occupation. They are kept women of fashion and as such were not welcome at the Salon. The dark-haired girl is in fact in a state of semi-undress. She lies in her petticoats, resting her head on her crumpled skirts, a cashmere shawl casually draped across her provocative frills.

As his later paintings of female nudes show, Courbet was drawn to erotic themes, and as the critics of his day perhaps recognized, this composition, for all its apparent innocence, is saturated in sensuality. The atmosphere is heavy and listless, and evokes the oppressive heat of a summer's afternoon before a storm. Only a trace of sky is glimpsed above the dense turquoise river, little light or air penetrates the trees, and the canvas is thickly filled with foliage, flesh and fabric. In this turgid world, activity becomes impossible. The plump, mindless women, swaddled in their shawls and petticoats, are immobilized by their indolence, beneath a suffocating layer of heavy paint.

Although this sketch came from the collection of the artist's sister, Juliette Courbet, some critics have doubted its authenticity, and suggested that it is a copy of the Petit Palais picture. When one sees how freely and vigorously it is painted, this seems impossible. The colouring of the landscape, and the dense, broken surface texture are entirely characteristic of Courbet, while the physical type and mental character of the girls are captured with absolute certainty.

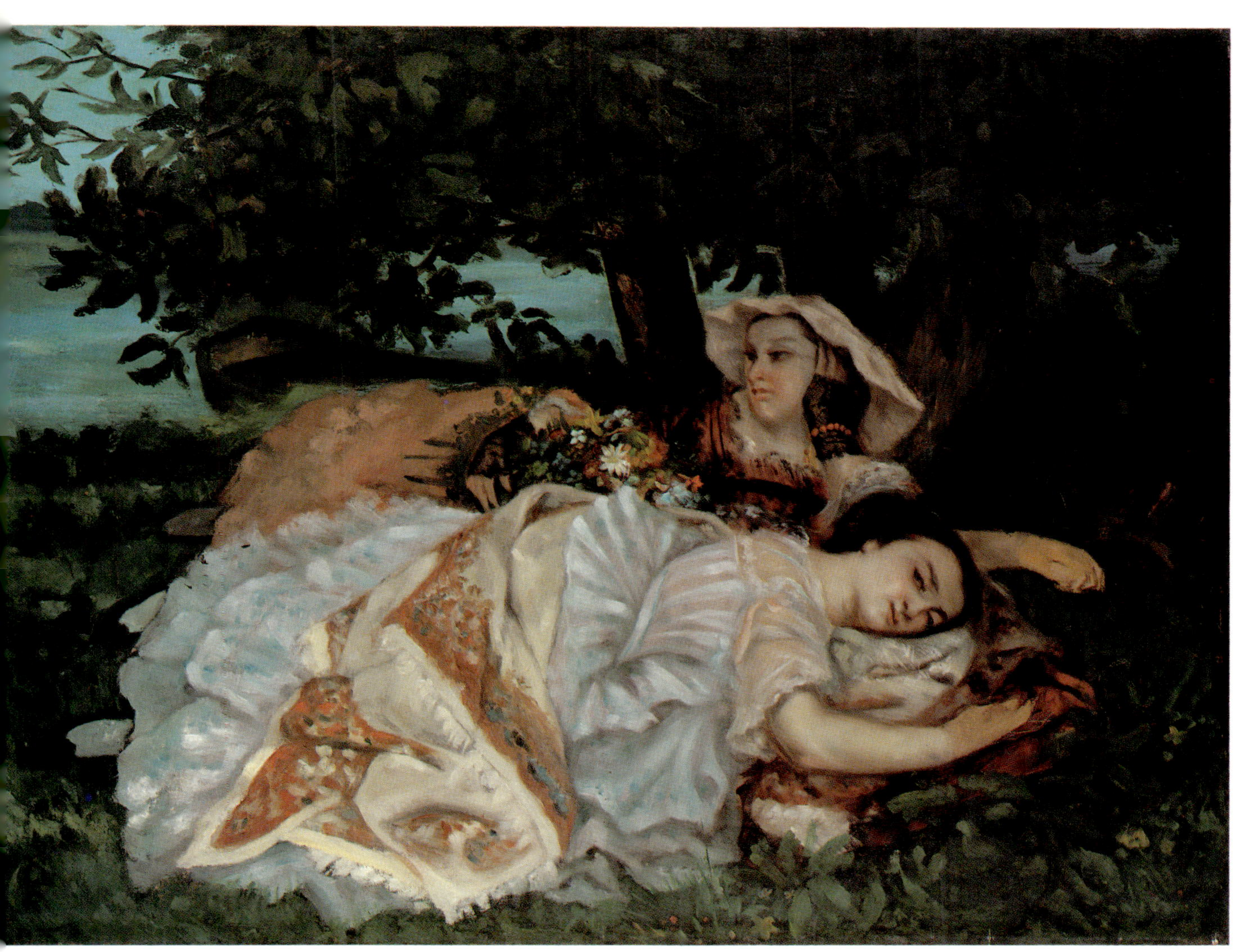

PLATE 12

Jean-Désiré-Gustave Courbet, 1819–1877

Still-Life with Apples and Pomegranate (No. 5983)

Signed: G. Courbet 71
Canvas, 44.5 × 61 cm
Purchased 1951

During the Franco-Prussian War of 1870–71, Courbet was elected chairman of the Arts Commission charged with the protection of works of art in and around Paris, and as such proposed that the Vendôme Column – regarded as a symbol of Napoleonic Imperialism – be dismantled. Subsequently, during the short-lived Paris Commune of 1871 in which Courbet served as a councillor, the Column was destroyed. In May 1871, after the Commune had been suppressed, Courbet was arrested, charged with, among other crimes, the destruction of the Column. On 2 September he was sentenced to six months' imprisonment and a fine of 500 francs. He was sent first to the prison of Saint-Pélagie in Paris and then on 30 December, on account of his deteriorating health, to the clinic of Dr Duval at Neuilly where he spent the remainder of his sentence on parole.

At Saint-Pélagie Courbet was visited by his sister Zoé who brought fruit and flowers which aroused in him a desire to paint, and when on 2 November he was given brushes and palette he began to paint a whole series of still-lifes. Although Courbet later maintained that he had painted most of these pictures of apples and flowers in prison – several are in fact inscribed with the name of the prison, Saint-Pélagie – he cannot have achieved much before moving to Neuilly. This little canvas of apples in a bowl is dated 1871 but it was almost certainly painted early in 1872 in the greater comfort of Dr Duval's clinic.

As a group the still-lifes are remarkably powerful and controlled. In the years before the War, Courbet had grown more open in his antagonism towards the Imperial Government, and his work had suffered in consequence, as it became loaded with provocative slights and increasingly careless in its execution. The violence and egoism which so often mar his paintings are here in the still-lifes held in check. Chastened by the ordeal of trial and imprisonment, and by his physical decline, Courbet devotes himself to the task of painting what he sees, and achieves an unaccustomed objectivity.

In the *Still-Life with Apples and Pomegranate* thick strokes of paint brilliantly convey the solidity of the mound of fruit and the rough texture of the earthenware bowl. And yet with what delicacy has he rendered the transparency of the glass and the dull gleam of the pewter jug. Only in long concentrated study of his subject is Courbet able to step out of himself and produce a picture which is arresting in its truth and integrity. Beyond perhaps the date, nothing is invented, nothing distorted by the need to proclaim a cause, justify an action or draw attention to his plight.

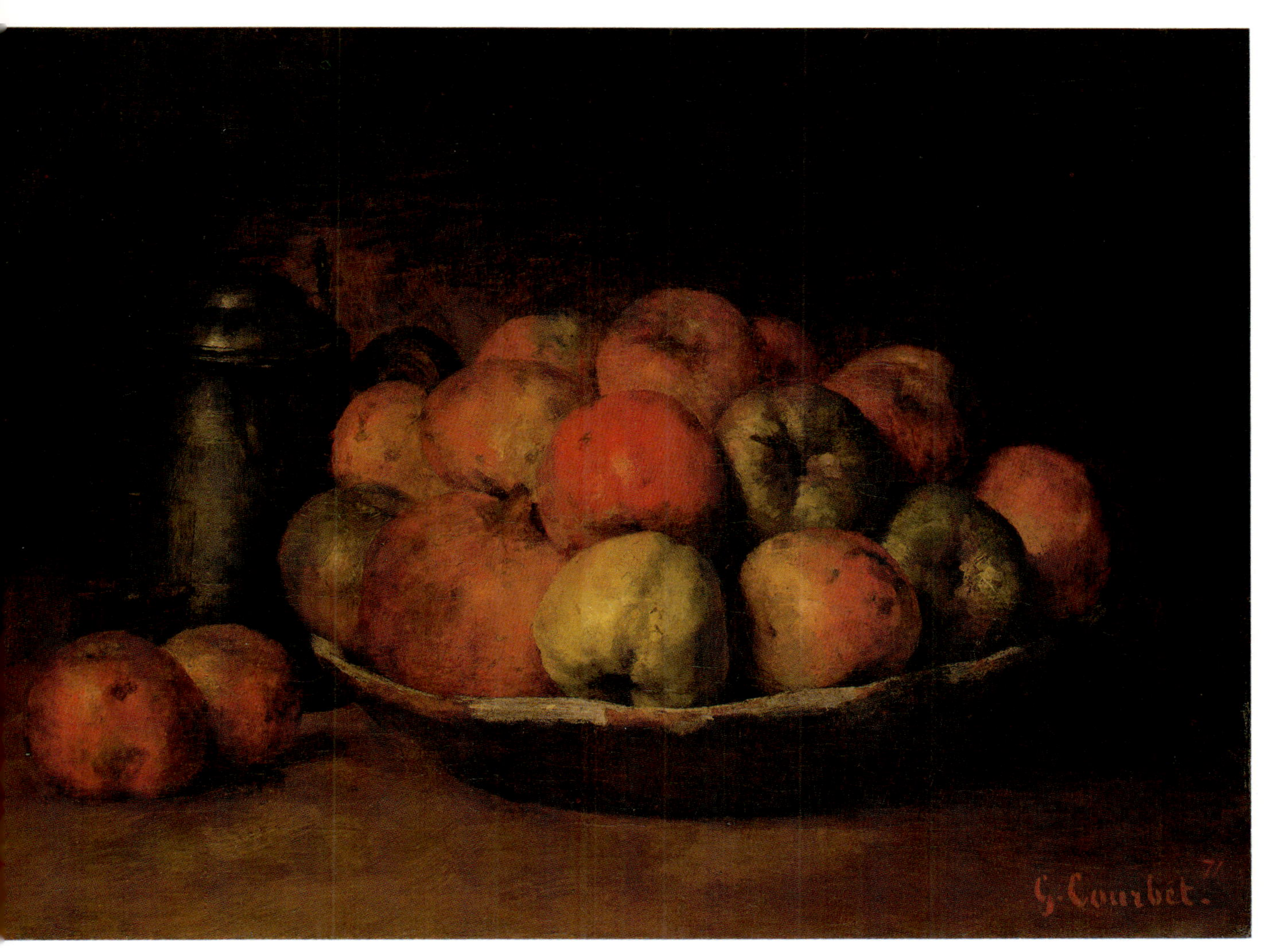
G. Courbet. 71

PLATE 13

Honoré-Victorin Daumier, 1808–1879

Don Quixote and Sancho Panza (No. 3244)

Oak, 40.3 × 64 cm.
Lane Bequest 1917

'One of the most important men in the whole of modern art' is how Baudelaire described his friend Daumier. Nevertheless during his lifetime Daumier's fame was based almost solely upon the caricatures which he was obliged to produce to earn his living. His paintings date for the most part from late in his career and were seen by only a small circle of admiring friends and artists. The originality of his powerful style is nevertheless due in no small part to his training as a caricaturist. As a graphic artist he was less constrained by academic theory than the painters who were obliged to win recognition at the Salon. He was expected to adopt the most expressive means at his disposal to poke fun at the institutions and characters of modern society. 'Look through his works,' wrote Baudelaire, 'and you will see parading before your eyes all that a great city contains of living monstrosities, in all their fantastic and thrilling reality.'

But underlying the satire is a deep vein of sympathy, so that when Daumier reveals the absurdities of human behaviour, it is without malice. He does so with the humility of someone who recognizes his own frailty. No wonder, then, that he chose later in life to illustrate Cervantes' story of Don Quixote. He had sent one painting on the subject to the Salon in 1850 and another dates from 1858. But in 1867 and 68, when he was almost sixty and beginning to lose his sight, he devoted himself to a whole series of pictures based upon the story. Perhaps he felt a certain affinity with the deluded old knight-errant. His ambition to be a painter had come to naught; and he had ended up in prison for his political beliefs. But in his down-to-earth common-sense and kindness, as well as in his portly build, Daumier was a Sancho Panza.

In this painting showing Don Quixote charging a flock of sheep, a working sketch for a more finished picture, Daumier has made much of the contrast between the long, lean Don Quixote (who elsewhere in his paintings looks as though he could have stepped out of an El Greco) and the corpulent Sancho Panza, the one mounted on a skeletal horse, the other on a stout donkey. As a caricaturist, Daumier was well versed in economy of means and here the whole absurd and poignant episode is conveyed without any detail. The composition is boldly massed out in a few broad areas of light and shade, with the shapes of Don Quixote and Sancho Panza expressively silhouetted against the sky, and the fluent under-drawing still showing through.

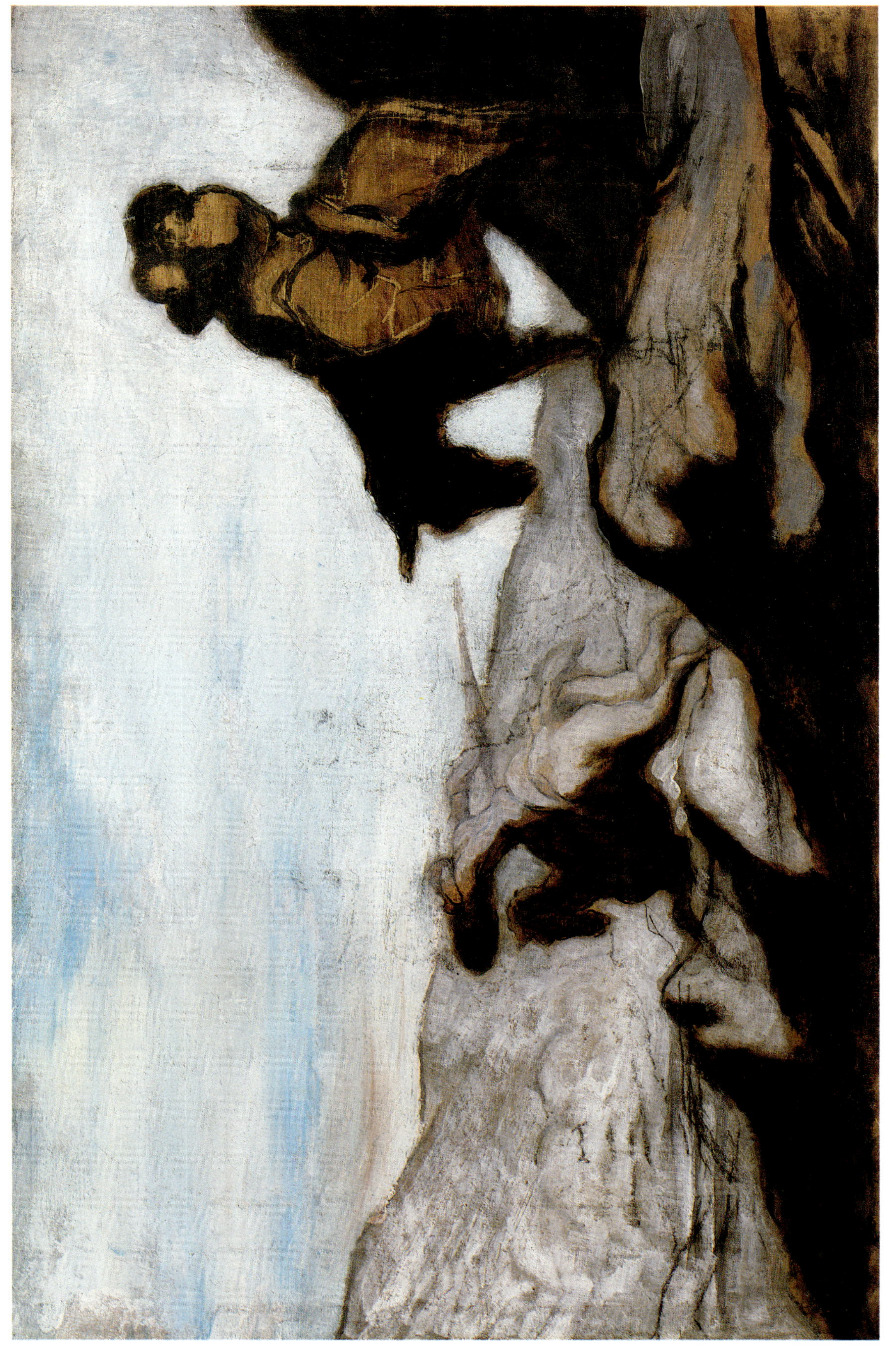

PLATE 14

Charles-François Daubigny, 1817–1878

Alders (No. 2623)

Signed: Daubigny 1872
Mahogany, 33 × 57 cm.
George Salting Bequest 1910

Daubigny was one of those very rare artists, like Boudin, who, prior to the Impressionists, worked in the open directly from nature. Yet the simplicity of his subject matter and liveliness of his rapid execution made him the butt of violent criticism when he exhibited at the Salon. 'It is really too bad that this landscape painter who possesses such a true, such a just, and such a natural feeling, is satisfied by an impression and neglects details to this extent,' complained Théophile Gautier, a critic usually well-disposed to innovatory talents. 'His pictures are but rough drafts, and very slightly developed . . . Each object is indicated by an apparent or real contour, but the landscapes of M. Daubigny offer merely spots of colour juxtaposed.'

During the early part of his career Daubigny made his way by engraving illustrations for book publishers. Not until 1848 did his painting attract the attention of the critics at the Salon. His early landscapes, like those of the Barbizon artists, Rousseau and Diaz, are precisely painted and full of fine detail. It was under the influence of Corot who became a firm friend in 1852 that he modified his style, sacrificing detail for greater fidelity to light and atmosphere, and subordinating subject matter to the depiction of natural effects, studied at close quarters in the open.

While the fresh execution of Daubigny's later works earned him the wrath of the critics, it won him the fervent admiration of younger painters, and especially of Monet and his Impressionist friends. In Daubigny Monet found another artist obsessed by the effect of light on water. They worked together in 1865 in the company of Courbet and Boudin at Trouville, and it was from Daubigny that Monet stole the idea of a studio-boat to enable him to paint on the river. Daubigny had constructed his, the *Botin*, in 1857 and continued to use it until his death, exploring the river Oise near his home at Auvers and painting views of the banks and water-meadows from his vantage point on the surface of the water.

This small picture of the river bank lined with alders may well have been painted from the *Botin*; no foreground shore breaks the expanse of dazzling water. In its fluent and fluid handling, high-keyed colouring and informal arrangement, it shows Daubigny at his best and most natural. The truthfulness of the sunset effect and the absolute sureness of tone and touch are the result of long experience of *plein-air* painting.

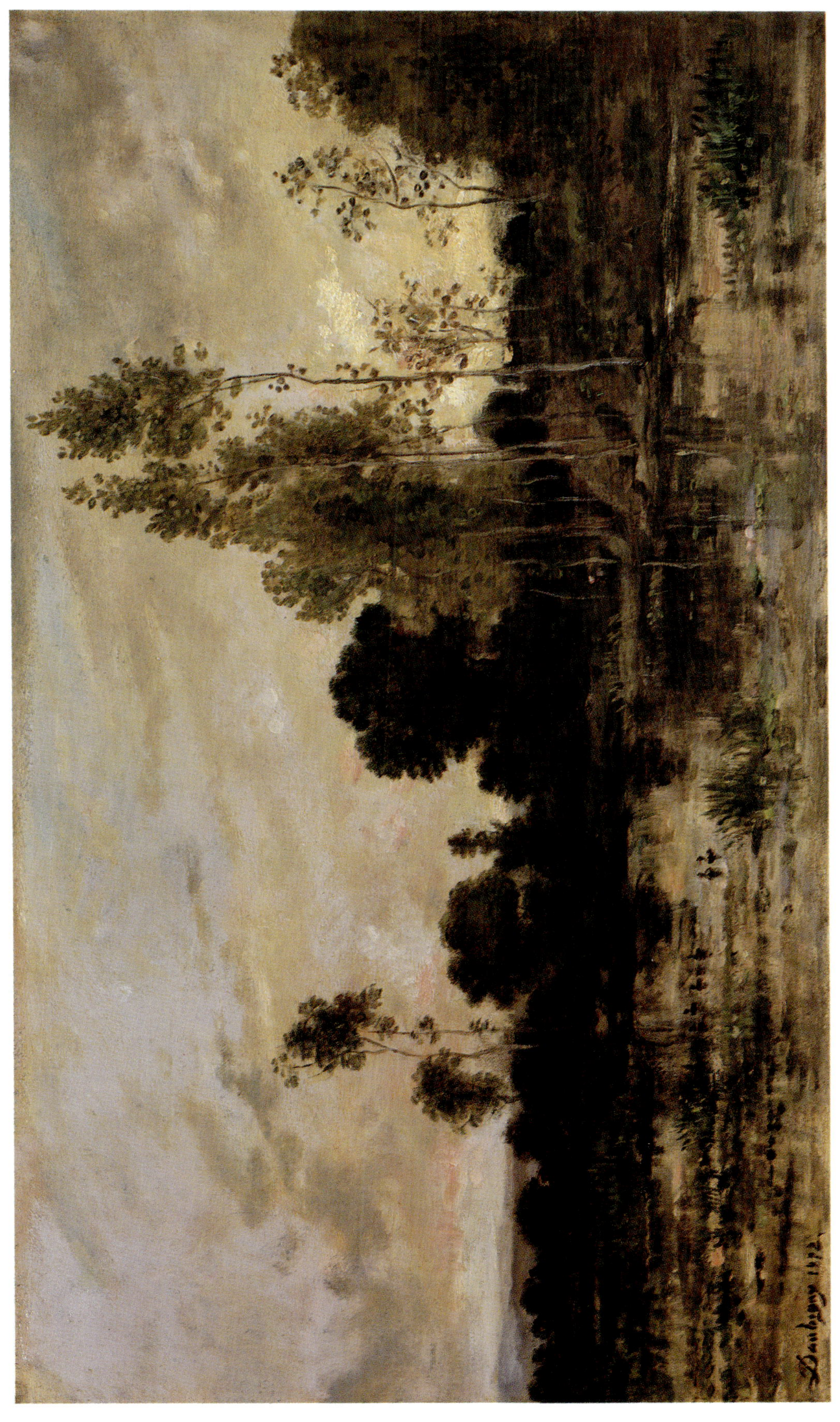

PLATE 15

Eugène-Louis Boudin, 1824–1898

The Beach at Trouville (No. 6309)

Signed: E. Boudin
Oak, 21.6 × 45.8 cm.
Bequeathed by Miss Judith E. Wilson, 1960

This little painting was once owned by Monet, the artist to whom Eugène Boudin had been a vital formative influence as well as a loyal friend. Monet frequently worked with Boudin, who encouraged him to paint in the open, directly from the motif (see Plate 21).

When Monet met him, however, in 1858, Boudin had still to make his reputation. Born in Honfleur, the son of a ship's captain, he inherited a lifelong love of the sea; nearly all his work was produced around the harbours and beaches of the Channel coast. When he was twenty he opened a framing shop in Le Havre to which came the numerous artists who spent their summers at the coast, including Couture, Troyon and Millet. On the encouragement of the latter, Boudin decided to become a painter, and except for a brief stay in Paris, trained himself by sketching directly from nature in the open, as Corot had done before him. 'The romantics have had their day,' Boudin remarked. 'Henceforth we must seek the simple beauties of nature . . . nature truly seen in all its variety, its freshness.'

The range of Boudin's art is extremely limited. He felt no need to travel, or to paint large eye-catching canvases. The local scenery around Le Havre offered him sufficient scope, and he worked conscientiously at his landscapes and seascapes, alone or in the company of Courbet, the Dutch artist Jongkind, and later, Monet. By the 1860s he had devised a rapid, free technique to capture the appearance of sea, sky and human activity, a notation of flecks and dabs of colour which in its ability to suggest atmosphere anticipates Impressionist painting.

In his pictures of the fashionable visitors who flocked to the resorts of the Channel coast during the leisurely years of the Second Empire, he discovered a hitherto untreated range of subjects which Courbet as well as Monet was to take up. Apart from capturing the light and atmosphere of the coast, Boudin found a place for the bourgeoisie in modern painting. 'The peasants have their painters of predeliction,' he wrote, 'but between ourselves, do not these middle-class men and women walking on the pier towards the setting sun have a right to be fixed on canvas?' In this painting families of visitors with nursemaids and children are informally disposed across a wide expanse of light-filled beach, the women wearing full-skirted crinolines which were fashionable in the 1860s, and carrying parasols which create accents of bright colour across the picture.

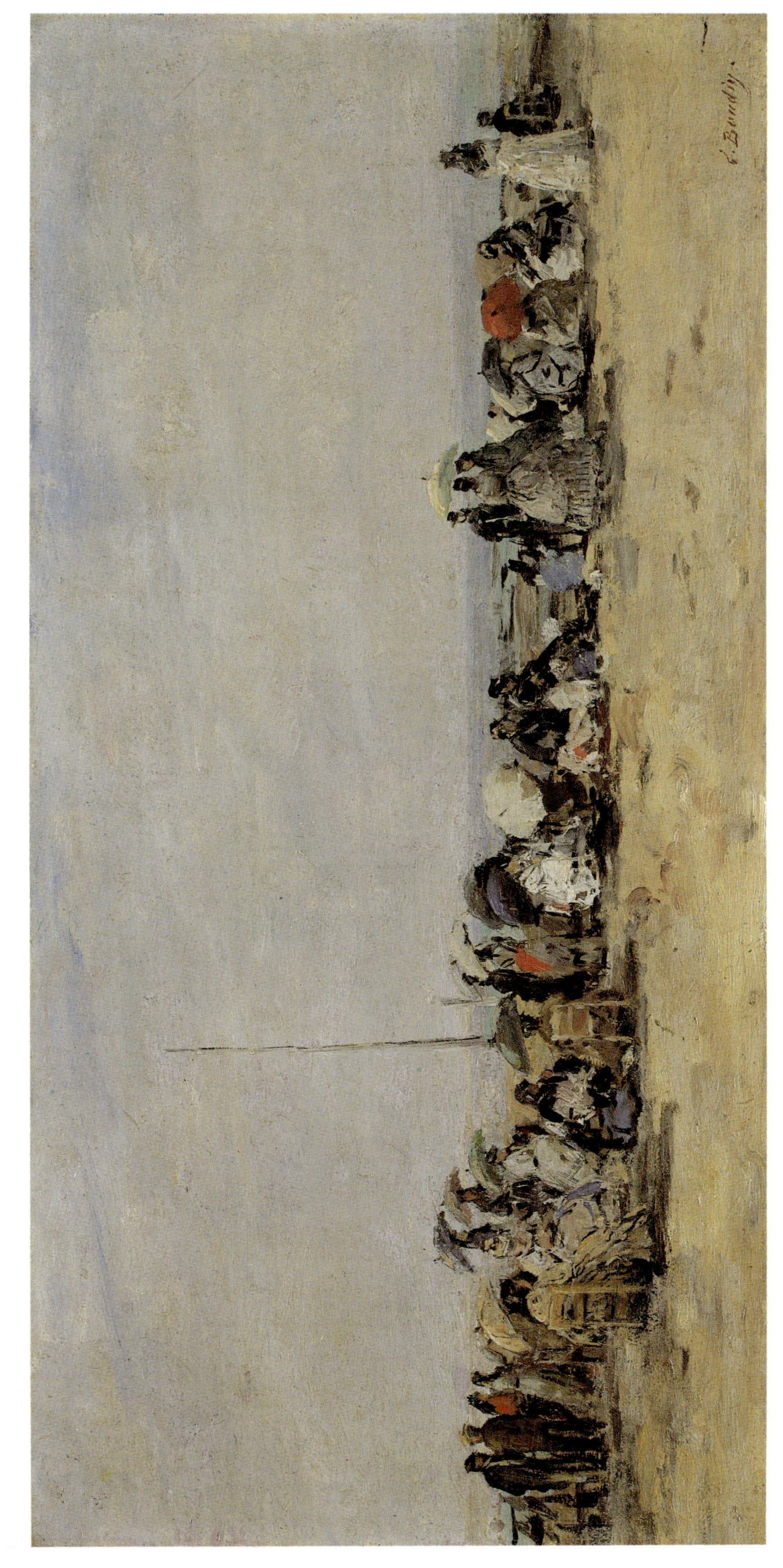

PLATE 16

Hilaire-Germain-Edgar Degas, 1834–1917

Young Spartans Wrestling (No. 3860)

Stamped: Degas
Canvas, 109 × 154 cm.
Purchased, Courtauld Fund, 1924

At first glance, one might easily assume that this odd painting, with its hot orange tone and archaic subject-matter, was a sketch by some neo-classical pupil of David. There is little about it that is obviously Impressionist. But if one looks a little further one can begin to discern the family resemblance between these skinny adolescents and the young 'rats' that Degas was later to show practising their movements or slumped at rest in the ballet rehearsal rooms in the rue Lepeletier. It is by no means as assured as the paintings of the 1870s; Degas clearly had some difficulty in arranging the girls in a satisfactory group; but there is already that characteristic preoccupation with bodies arrested in mid-movement, their arms and legs frozen in gestures that are both natural and expressive.

The subject of Degas' picture, however, still conforms to the expectations of the Classical School and the Salon. When he exhibited it at the Impressionist exhibition of 1880, twenty years after it was painted, Degas described it as *Young Spartan Girls challenging some Boys*. He derived the theme, which had already been treated by other nineteenth-century painters, from the Roman historian Plutarch, who in his *Life of Lycurgus* describes how the Spartan legislator ordered girls to engage in contests of wrestling. An entry in one of Degas' notebooks reads: 'young girls and young boys wrestling in the Plane-tree grove, under the eye of the aged Lycurgus, beside the mothers'. In the background of Degas' picture stands the group of Lycurgus and the Spartan mothers, and beyond them still a landscape with the city of Sparta, and the precipitous rock from which malformed Spartan infants were thrown.

As a student of Louis Lamothe, a respected classical painter and former pupil of Ingres, Degas would have been expected to produce works of this kind. Others of his early compositions treat such subjects as *The Daughter of Jephtha* and *Semiramis founding Babylon*. The emphasis on anatomical drawing and the rather flat colour are typical of the school of Ingres. When Degas met the elderly artist in 1855 he was urged to 'draw lines young man, many lines, from memory or from nature'. But Degas has left his picture unfinished, mapped out in coarsely-worked paint, with changes of pose still showing. And entirely alien to orthodox academic painting are the commonplace faces and figures of the protagonists who confront each other with all the ill-mannered surliness of a gang of schoolchildren. Degas is more interested in the young models off the Paris streets who posed for him, than in the ideal of high-minded Spartan youth that was his purported subject. From here it is but a short distance to the paintings of jockeys, ballet-dancers, laundresses and shop girls – the unidealized types of the contemporary world.

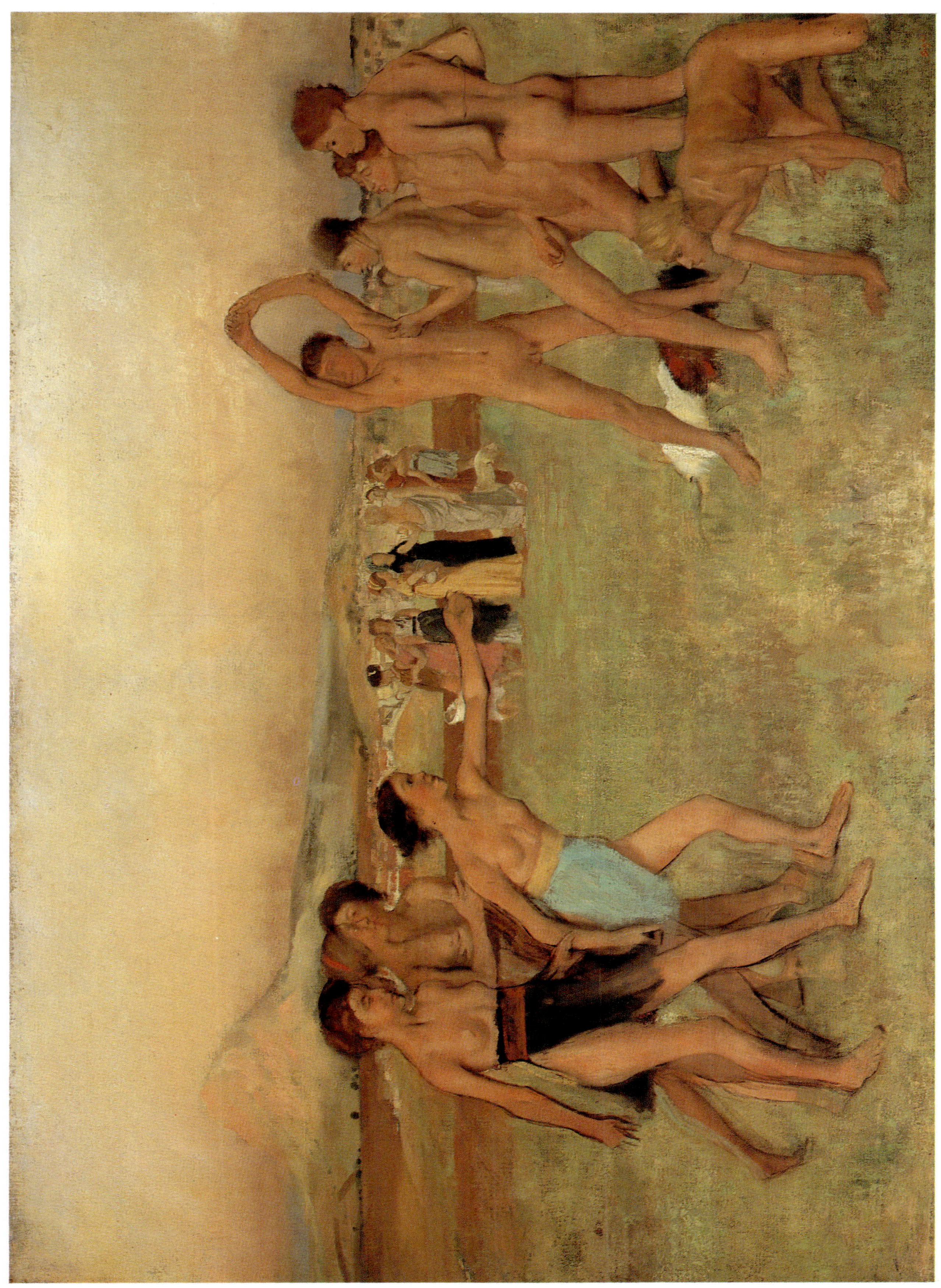

PLATE 17

Edouard Manet, 1832–1883

Music in the Tuileries Gardens (No. 3260)

Signed: éd Manet 1862
Canvas, 76 × 118 cm.
Lane Bequest 1917

Music in the Tuileries Gardens, which Manet exhibited at the Galerie Martinet in March 1863, is the artist's first major painting of modern city life. The subject, a crowd of fashionable Parisians gathered in the gardens of the Tuileries palace to hear the band, offers Manet the opportunity to depict a whole milieu: that of the wealthy bourgeoisie of the Second Empire. This milieu was his own – his father was an eminent magistrate – and he has depicted himself, on the extreme left of the picture, with many of his friends dotted among the crowd. Standing beside Manet is the painter Albert de Balleroy, with whom Manet shared a studio, and seated just to their right is the sculptor and critic Zacharie Astruc, whose portrait Manet painted. The two seated women are said to be Madame Loubens and Madame LeJosne, and the knot of three men behind them are the poets Baudelaire and Gautier with possibly Baron Taylor. To the left of Baudelaire can be seen the head of the painter Fantin-Latour, who, in 1867, painted Manet's portrait. The standing top-hatted figure, just right of centre, is Manet's brother, Eugène, and immediately to his right against the tree is the composer of popular operettas, Jacques Offenbach. Others of the assembled company may include the journalist Aurélien Scholl, the painter Charles Monginot and the critic Champfleury.

Situated in the gardens adjacent to the Emperor's palace, Manet's elegant gathering has a courtly feel, and the informal arrangement and stylish poses are partly borrowed from a little picture of cavaliers in the Louvre, then thought to be by Velázquez, which Manet copied. Manet's painting also owes much to less aristocratic sources, to the popular prints of the eighteenth century and the illustrated journals of his own day depicting gatherings in public parks. But perhaps the most significant influence on the picture came from his friend Baudelaire, who appears in it, and who, we are told, was Manet's 'habitual companion' when he 'went almost everyday to the Tuileries, making studies in the open, under the trees, after the children who played, and the groups of nurses who rested on the seats'. For over a decade Baudelaire had called for an artist to interpret the 'heroism of modern life', and his essay *The Painter of Modern Life*, which he completed shortly before Manet painted his picture, called for a modern treatment of contemporary urban themes. Manet's painting is daringly brief and allusive, so much so that it provoked outrage when it was exhibited at the Galerie Martinet. Parts appear unfinished, faces are left flat and unmodelled, the trees are scraped on with a palette-knife, and in spite of the fact that we know Manet spent much time planning and executing the picture, it has all the appearance of being effortlessly achieved. Apart from creating a compelling pictorial whole, Manet in this way flaunts a nonchalance which is the hall-mark of the sophisticated society he depicts.

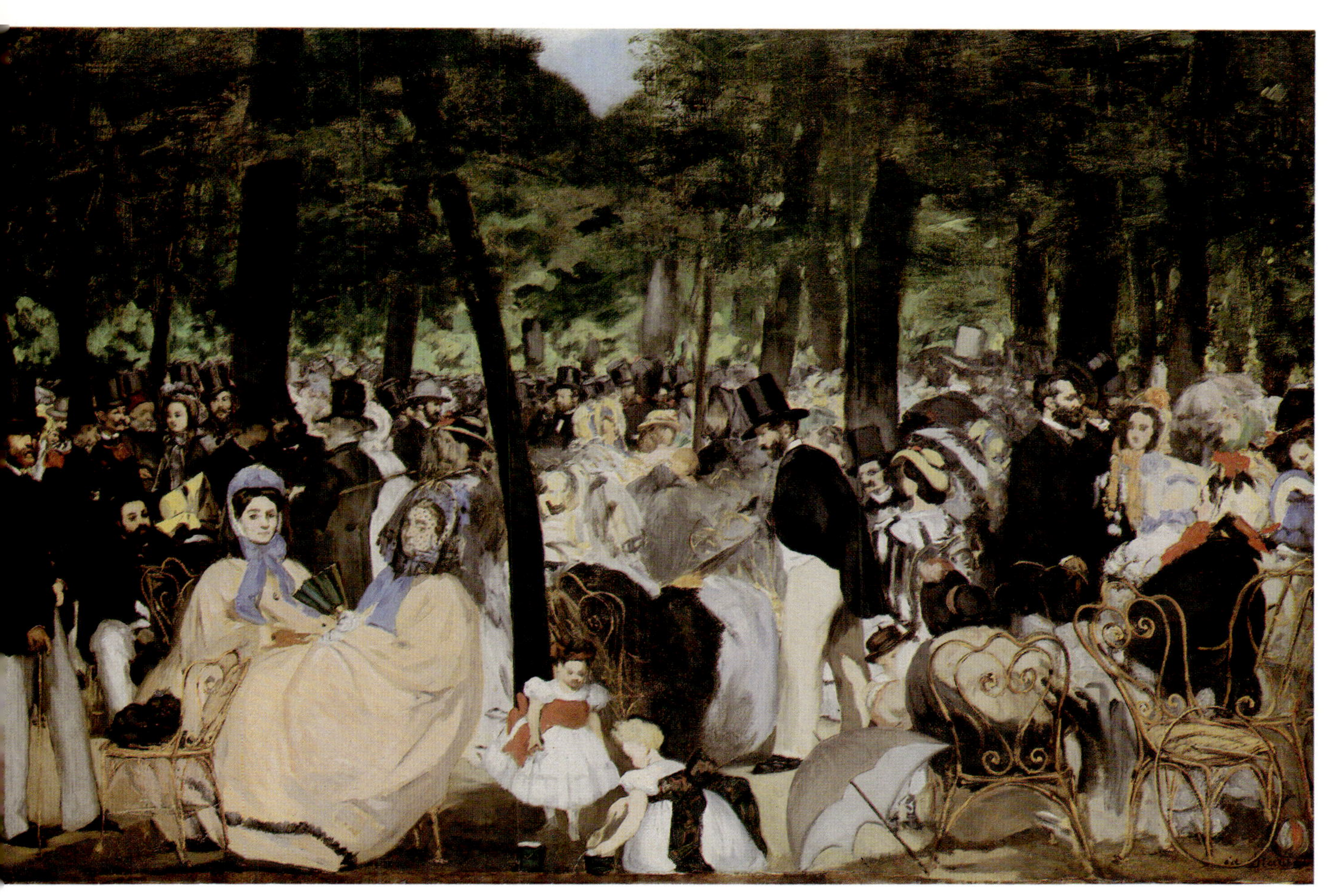

PLATE 18

Edouard Manet, 1832–1883

The Execution of Maximilian (No. 3294)

Four canvas fragments: 190 × 160, 99 × 59, 89 × 30, 35 × 26 cm. Purchased 1918

The National Gallery version of *The Execution of Maximilian* has suffered an unfortunate history. Probably abandoned by Manet before its completion, it remained in his studio where it rapidly deteriorated. The left-hand section, which would have shown Maximilian and the second of the two generals with whom he was executed, was cut away and destroyed within Manet's lifetime. The remainder, by the time of his death, had suffered such paint losses that it was cut up and sold in parts. However, Manet's friend, the painter Degas, succeeded in acquiring all the surviving pieces and stuck them down on a single canvas. It was in this form that they were purchased by the Gallery at the Degas sale, but once more they were separated and exhibited individually, and only in recent years have they again been displayed as a whole.

On 19 June 1867 the Emperor of Mexico, Maximilian, was shot by firing squad at Querétaro after the city had fallen to Juárez's nationalist forces. The quixotic Hapsburg archduke had accepted the Mexican throne in 1864 at the instigation of Napoleon III of France, but at the beginning of 1867 the French Emperor withdrew all French troops from Mexico leaving Maximilian without support in the face of rising nationalist opposition.

The political background to the death of Maximilian helps to explain why Manet devoted so much time in 1867 and early 1868 to a series of paintings commemorating the event. The news of the execution was widely reported in the French press and it was generally held that Maximilian was the innocent victim of Louis-Napoleon's bungled foreign policy. A staunch Republican in politics, Manet would have shared the outrage at these scandalous and tragic events.

He produced four paintings of the execution: the earliest is a canvas in Boston; that is followed by the damaged National Gallery version; then Manet probably painted the sketch in Copenhagen; and finally he painted the huge version in Mannheim, in which the execution takes place against a wall instead of an open landscape. For the concept, Manet was indebted to Goya's *3rd May 1808* in the Prado, but the details of the execution and the features of Maximilian and the two generals who died with him, Tomás Mejía and Miguel Miramón, he took from contemporary photographs and newspaper accounts. However, he has shown the firing squad in French uniforms. He is said to have had soldiers from a local barracks pose for him, but the reason for this apparent oversight may be that Manet wished to imply that Maximilian's executioner was in effect the treacherous Napoleon III. Nevertheless, Manet's soldiers perform their duty without any display of emotion. He deliberately avoids any suggestion of melodrama, and with restrained understatement heightens the pathos of the execution.

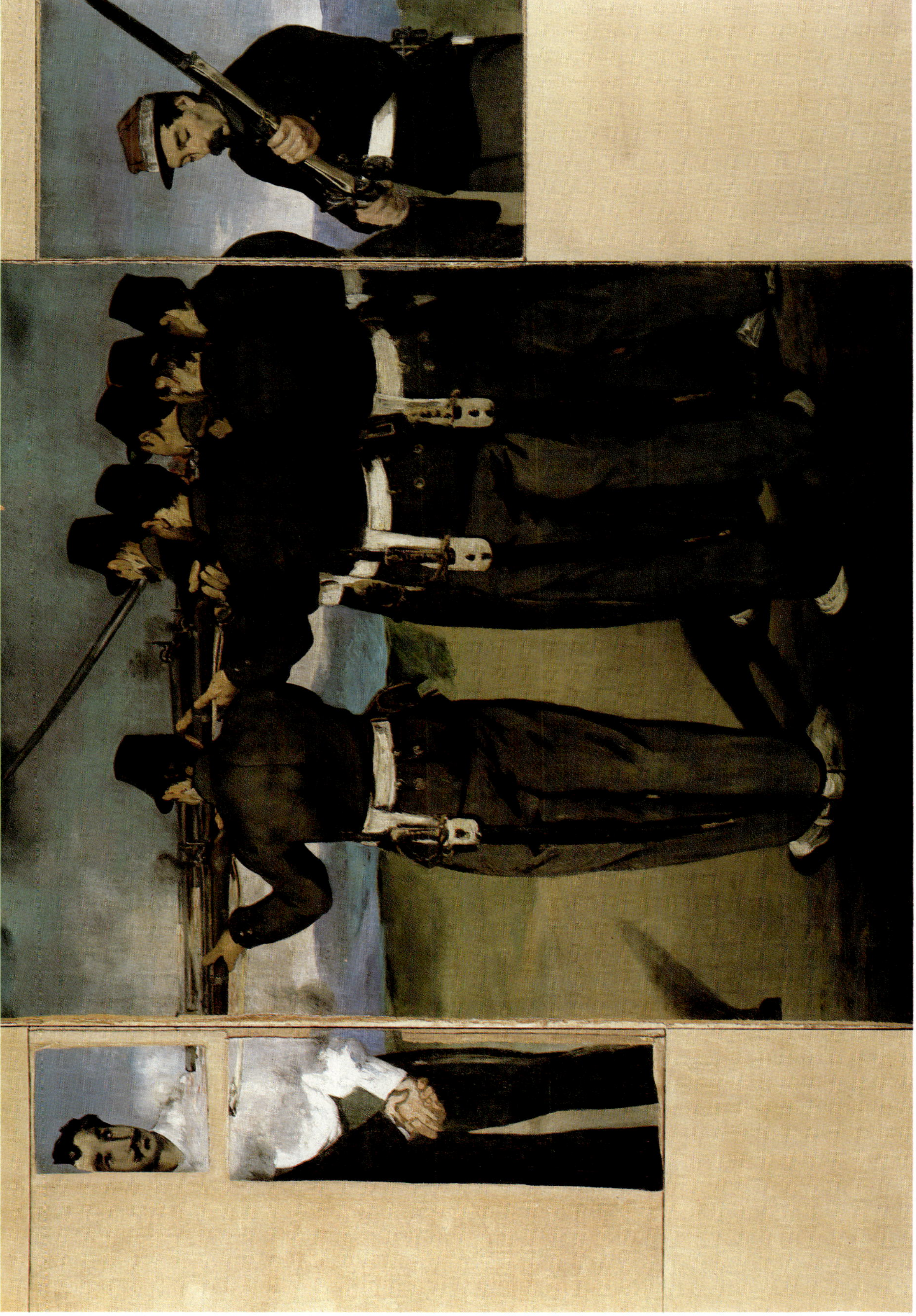

PLATE 19

Claude-Oscar Monet, 1840–1926

Bathers at La Grenouillère (No. 6456)

Signed: Claude Monet 1862
Canvas, 73 × 92 cm.
Richard and Sophie Walzer bequest, 1979

In the summer of 1869 Monet was living with his mistress Camille and young son Jean at Saint-Michel, a hamlet near Bougival, west of Paris, in conditions of extreme hardship. He was without money to eat, let alone paint; but his friend Bazille sent him canvases, and Renoir brought him scraps filched from his parents' table. Monet wanted to paint a picture for the next Salon, depicting the riverside café of La Grenouillère. In August he wrote to Bazille, 'I do indeed have a dream, a picture, the bathing-place at La Grenouillère, for which I have made some bad studies, but it is a dream. Renoir, who has just spent two months here, wants to do this picture too.' The picture was painted, but the Salon jury of 1870 rejected it and subsequently it disappeared. What Monet called his 'bad studies' survive, however: one in the Metropolitan Museum, New York, showing the little island called, because of its shape, the '*camembert*' or '*pot aux fleurs*', with the floating café on the right; the other, this painting recently acquired by the National Gallery, showing the bathing-cabins, rowing-boats moored at the bank, and the narrow cat-walk leading to the '*camembert*'. Renoir, working alongside Monet, produced paintings of almost identical views.

Situated on the wooded Île de Croissy, La Grenouillère was a popular bathing and boating resort during the 1860s and 70s, particularly among the factory workers from the nearby industrial suburbs. It was hardly smart. Apparently it took its name, meaning 'frog-pond', from the women of easy virtue who patronized the place and were known in Second Empire parlance as 'frogs'. Nevertheless it provided Monet with the kind of animated river-scene he liked to paint.

Why he should have called his sketches 'poor' is a mystery. Maybe it was merely casual self-depreciation, or perhaps a passing acknowledgement of the difficulty of his task – to depict the gamut of human activity and the action of light, brilliant here, subdued there, filtering through the trees and reflected on the water. This sketch is laid in with great speed. Broad brushstrokes and slabs of pure colour are all it has taken to describe the varied forms of bathers thrashing in the water or seated on the banks, gaudily dressed strollers, brightly painted rowing-boats and rippling waves reflecting the afternoon sky and heavy summer foliage. Perhaps he was surprised at his own boldness. There is nothing here of the customary finish of an exhibition picture, and it is far broader than his earlier *plein-air* studies. It is, in effect, one of the first Impressionist paintings, in which an overall texture of fragmented brushstrokes of bright colour is used to convey the light and atmosphere of the outdoors, and to evoke the warmth, noise and movement which paint cannot depict.

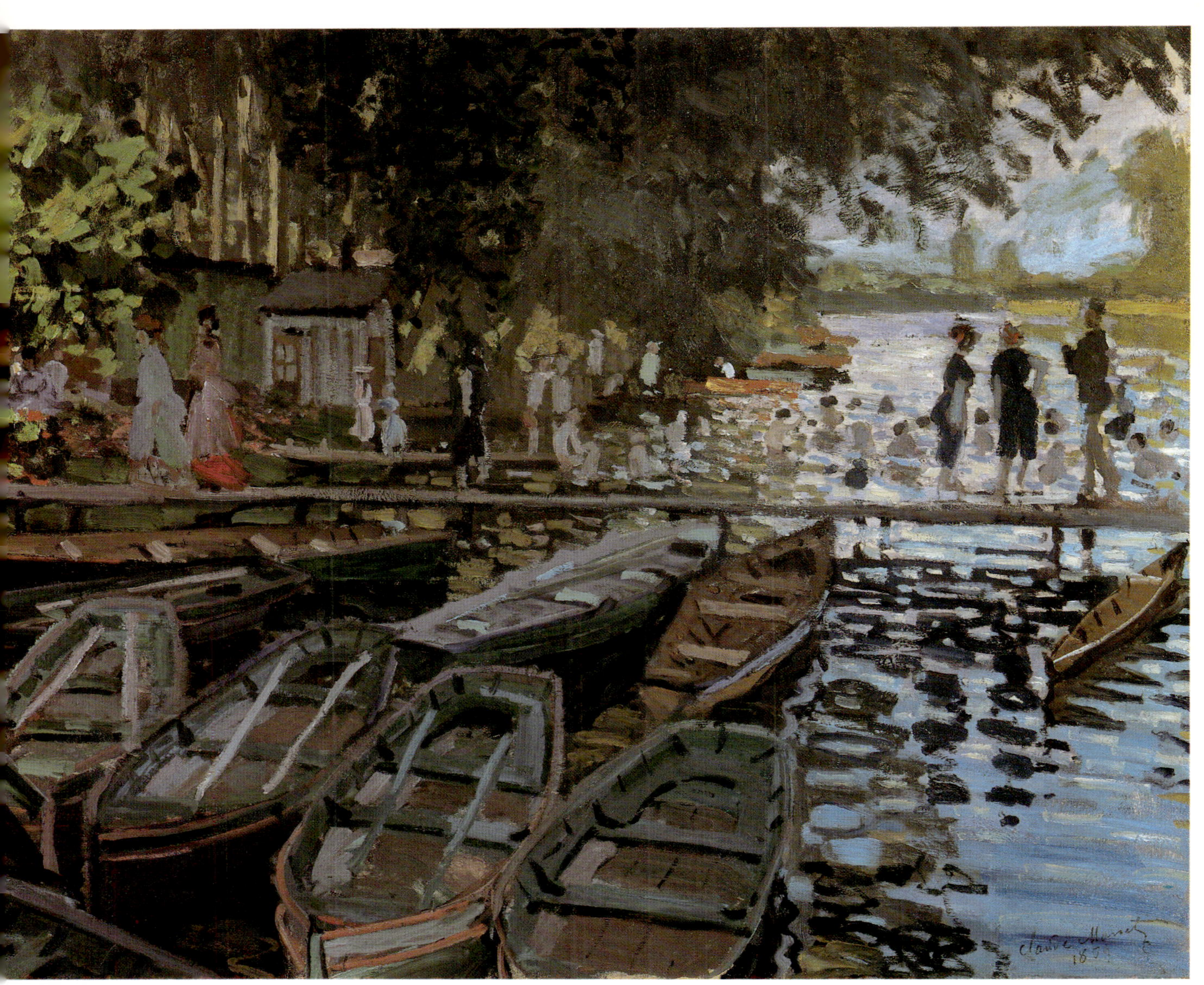

PLATE 20

Camille Pissarro, 1830–1903

View from Louveciennes (No. 3265)

Signed: C. Pissarro
Canvas, 52 × 82 cm.
Lane Bequest 1917

Pissarro was the oldest of the Impressionist painters and his artistic origins are firmly rooted in the earlier landscape painting of Corot and Daubigny. In 1857, shortly after he arrived in Paris from his native St Thomas in the Danish West Indies, he was introduced to Corot, who urged him to paint direct from nature. Subsequently he abandoned his formal training to paint in the open in the company of other disciples of Corot, and at the Académie Suisse in Paris, where in 1859 he met Monet.

As a landscape painter Pissarro was more concerned than Monet or Sisley with pictorial structure and rather less daring in his use of colour. This spring landscape, painted probably in 1870, for example, is for all its apparent simplicity a carefully composed painting and shows how thoroughly Pissarro had absorbed the lessons of Corot. It is firmly divided into horizontal bands, establishing a clear recession into space; the elements of the landscape – the larger framing trees at each side, the Aqueduc de Marly silhouetted on the hill to the left, and the cluster of houses at the hamlet of Voisins in the centre – are judiciously disposed to create a satisfying arrangement; and the colour is soft-toned, tending towards neutral greens and earth colours, and applied with restraint. The carefully placed figures particularly recall Corot. A peasant woman with a white bonnet, a workman in shirt-sleeves, and a distant waggon add lively accents to the composition, but remain impersonal enough not to disturb the tranquil tenor of the scene.

Nevertheless Pissarro was not content merely to repeat the formulae of his predecessors. In 1869, shortly before he painted this view, he had moved from Pontoise, just north-west of Paris, to the village of Louveciennes, near Bougival and Chatou to the west of Paris. He there found himself close to his young friends Monet, Renoir and Sisley who were moving away from the examples of Corot and Courbet towards a less formally structured kind of landscape painting, executed as far as possible in the open, in which light was to provide the chief motif. Already in Pissarro's view of the outskirts of Louveciennes, the picture surface is more fragmented by fine strokes and dabs of paint than in any oil study of Corot, giving the illusion of light playing on newly budded hedgerows and through the bare spring branches. With this new-found freedom of handling, the structure of the picture begins to dissolve, creating a feeling of transparency and filling the canvas with air.

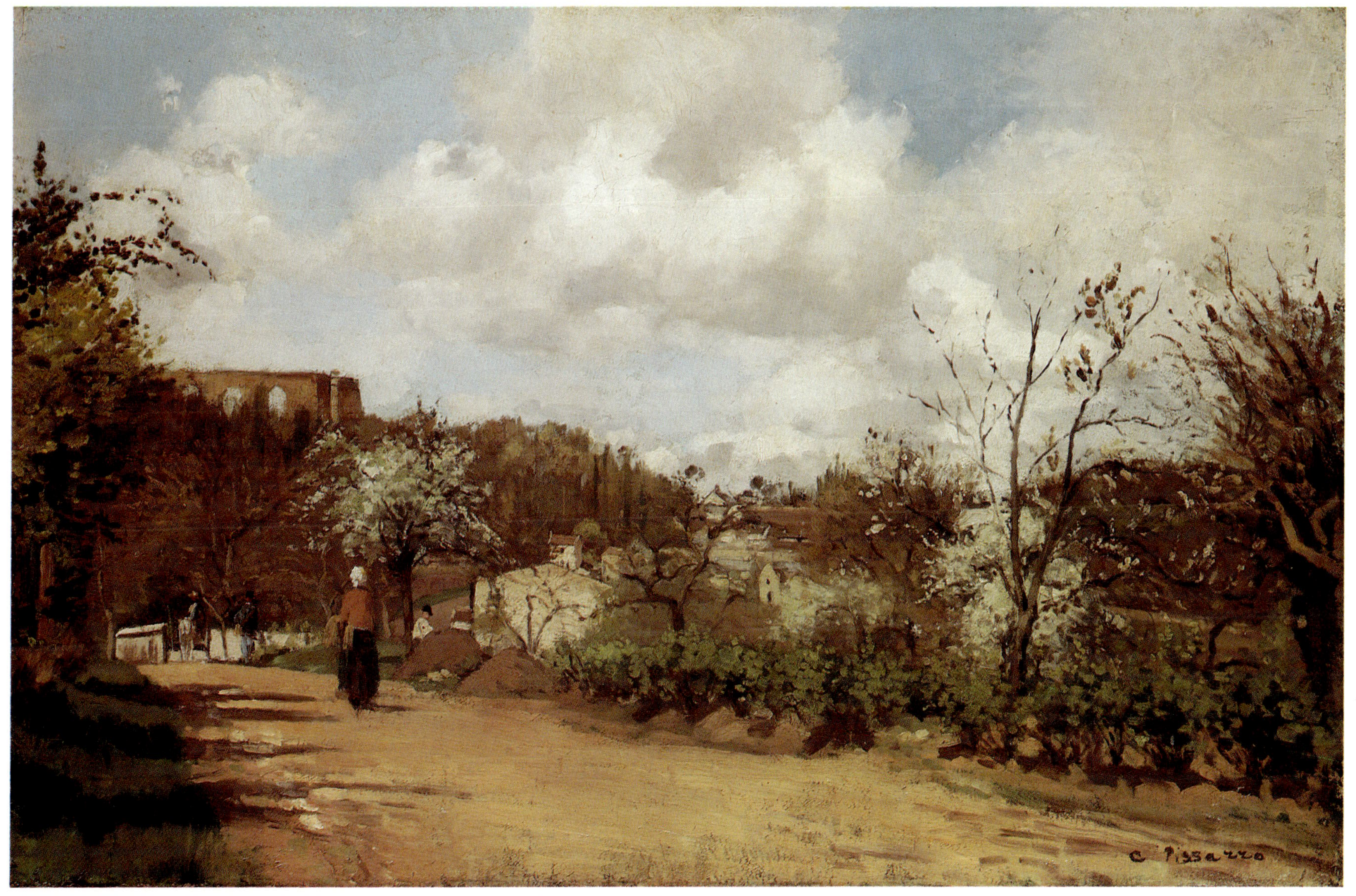
C. Pissarro

PLATE 21

Claude-Oscar Monet, 1840–1926

The Beach at Trouville (No. 3951)

Signed: Cl.M.70
Canvas, 37.5 × 45.7 cm.
Purchased, Courtauld Fund, 1924

When France declared war on Prussia in July 1870 Monet was enjoying a productive stay at Trouville on the Channel coast in the company of his wife, Camille, and Eugène Boudin and his wife. Although by 1870 he had enjoyed only limited success at the Paris Salon, the pictures he painted at Trouville display enormous skill and confidence.

His companion at Trouville, the painter Eugène Boudin, had been his friend and mentor since they met in 1857, and often they had worked together, painting in the open at various coastal locations near Le Havre. 'Boudin, with untiring kindness, undertook my education,' Monet later acknowledged. 'My eyes were finally opened and I really understood nature; I learned at the same time to love it.'

Boudin's own work was rooted in the practice of painting directly from nature. He was largely self-taught and the pictures he painted of the Normandy beaches are chiefly of modest dimensions, have all the high tone of open-air sketches, and show fashionable holidaymakers seated or standing together in informal groups (see Plate 15). Monet soon overtook his teacher in daring and skill, but although his studies took him to Paris into other company, he still liked to return to his early haunts, to try to capture the light effects of the coast.

This sketch of Camille, whom he had married on 28 June, and a second woman who may be Madame Boudin, is entirely different in conception to Boudin's beach scenes. The holidaymakers in Boudin's paintings are always seen at a comfortable distance and become a feature of the landscape. In Monet's, the women are shown at close quarters. The artist is part of the same intimate group and we get a powerful sensation of what it is to sit on the beach in the dazzling midday sun with a brisk sea breeze. And Monet's sketch is painted with extraordinary breadth and freedom, achieving the maximum effect with the minimum detail. A few broad strokes suffice to sketch in the beach with its tent and chairs, a couple of distant figures, the two women with their parasols, and the light-filled sky. A dramatic change of tone marks the line of a veil across Camille's face, while a single dark brushstroke defines the position of her arm. In some places the paint barely covers the canvas; in the bright highlights on Camille's dress and across the back of the chair it is laid on in thick white slabs. The shadows are clear and luminous, and if further proof were necessary, grains of sand embedded in the surface are evidence that the picture was painted on the spot.

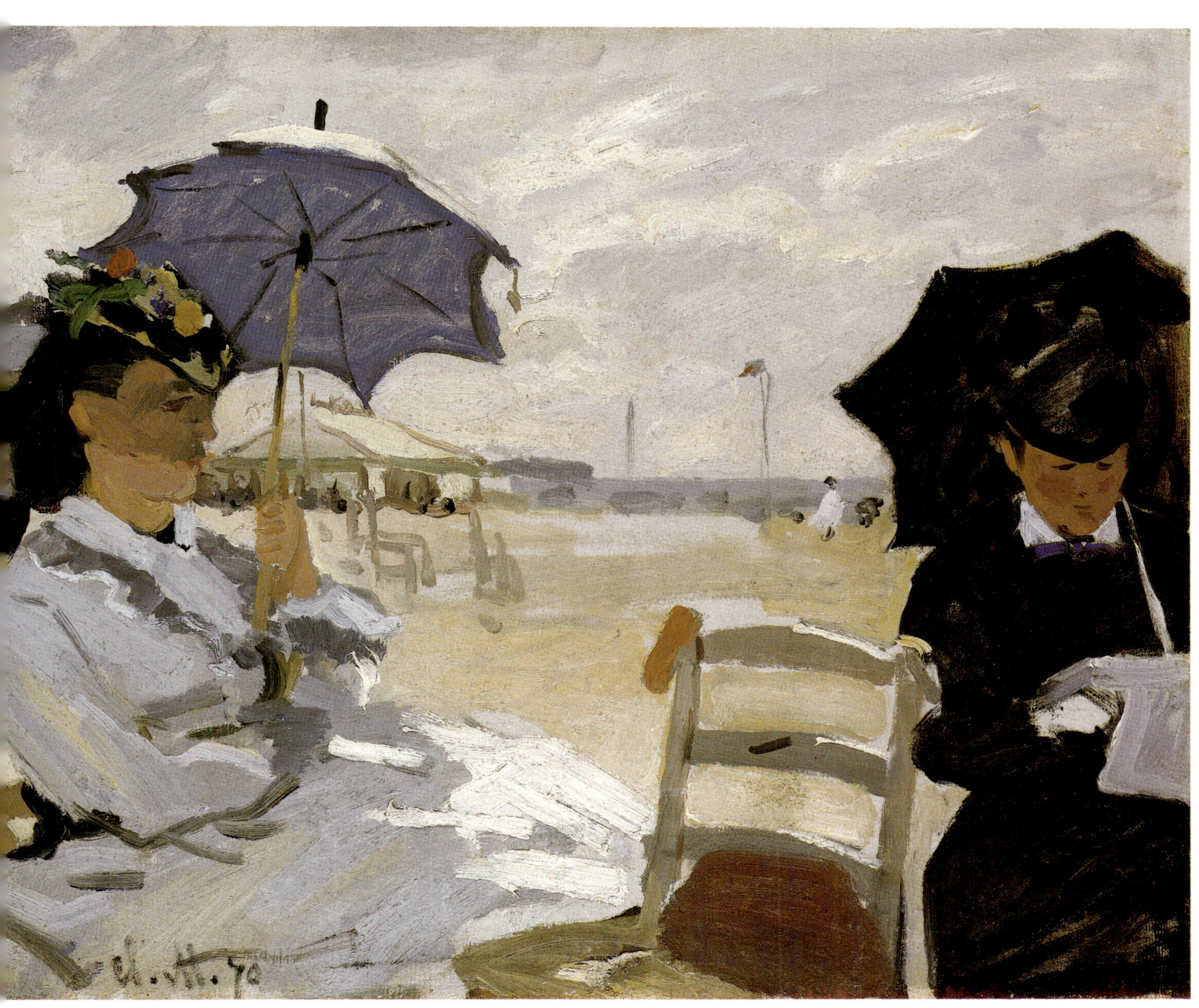

PLATE 22

Camille Pissarro, 1830–1903

Lower Norwood under Snow (No. 6351)

Signed: C. Pissarro '70
Canvas, 35.3 × 45.7 cm.
Presented by Viscount and Viscountess Radcliffe, 1964

The peaceful mood of this little landscape belies the dramatic events that surround its origin. Although so like the suburban views Pissarro painted at Louveciennes (see Plate 20), it represents a scene in South London, where Pissarro and his family fled following the outbreak of the Franco-Prussian War in 1870. Driven from their home at Louveciennes, which was turned into a butcher's shop by the invading Prussians, they took refuge first in Brittany with Pissarro's friend Piette, and subsequently in England, Pissarro being unable to fight for France owing to his Danish nationality. At Louveciennes he left behind his life's work, the greater part of which was destroyed.

Nevertheless London offered more than a refuge. There he met the dealer Paul Durand-Ruel who began to buy his pictures and put him in touch with Monet, who, unbeknown to Pissarro, had likewise escaped to the safety of England. London made a great impression on them both, and together they visited the museums and galleries where they became acquainted with the work of the English landscape painters – above all Turner, Constable and Crome. The pictures they painted during their stay were confident and adventurous. 'Monet and I were very enthusiastic over the London landscapes,' Pissarro later recalled. But the subjects they chose were quite different: 'Monet worked in the parks, whilst I, living in Lower Norwood, at that time a charming suburb, studied the effect of fog, snow and springtime.'

Among the pictures Pissarro painted in south London during the winter of 1870/71 are one of the station at Lordship Lane (a picture perhaps inspired by Turner's *Rain, Steam and Speed* in the National Gallery), one of the Crystal Palace, at the site near Sydenham to which it was moved after the Great Exhibition of 1851, and this little view of a street in Lower Norwood lightly powdered with snow. The broad, sketchy treatment suggests that it was painted entirely in the open, as also does the fidelity of atmosphere. The sky is pale and luminous, and the whole landscape is penetrated by light, so that with the lively touches of red, green and blue the winter scene becomes unexpectedly colourful.

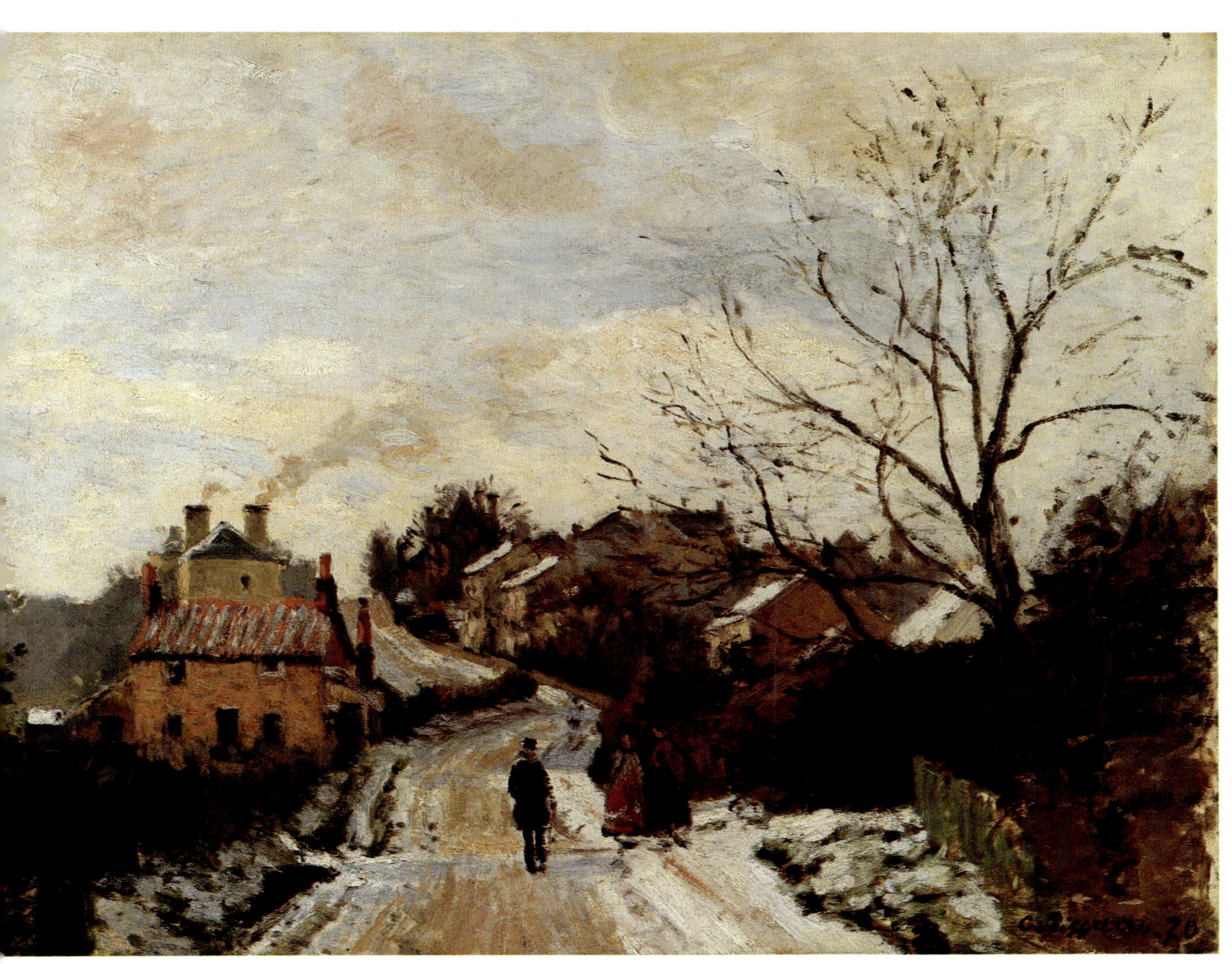

PLATE 23

Claude-Oscar Monet, 1840–1926

The Thames below Westminster (No. 6399)

Signed: Claude Monet 71
Canvas, 47 × 72 cm.
Bequeathed by Lord Astor of Hever, 1971

Like Pissarro, Monet had escaped the worst effects of the Franco-Prussian War by fleeing to London. While Paris lay under siege during the winter of 1870/71, Pissarro was busy painting the suburbs of South London, where the new rows of Victorian villas were rapidly encroaching on the countryside; and Monet, finding a taste of the country in the heart of the city, painted views of Hyde Park. But as in France, he was also drawn to the river, and painted several canvases of the Thames, busy with barges and tugs.

Earlier in the century London had played a significant part in the development of other French painters, notably Géricault and Delacroix, but the smoke-filled city would be expected to hold few attractions for the landscape painter. Monet, however, eagerly grasped any opportunity to undertake unusual motifs, and the smoggy atmosphere of London provided him with novel effects for his paintings. His view of Westminster Bridge and the Houses of Parliament is almost bleached of colour. A glimmer of spring sunshine just tinges the river and the sky with pink. A veil of cloud and smoke is cast over the buildings so that they emerge as ghost images against the pale, featureless sky. In this two-dimensional world a wooden pier projects into the river from the recently constructed Victoria Embankment, its dark beams silhouetted against the misty distance, forming a flat pattern of horizontals and verticals. To the modern eye this little corner of the canvas looks like nothing so much as a Mondrian, but for Monet's contemporaries the closest analogy would have been the Japanese print. In constructing his flattened river view, in which the whole field of the canvas is divided up and marked off by an almost abstract network of vertical and horizontal lines, Monet recalled the prints of 'the floating world' which had become all the rage in Paris during the previous decade, prints of Japanese bridges and wooden frame houses with screens and balconies overlooking flatly patterned landscapes. He might also have remembered the work of another admirer of Japanese Art, whose mistily monochromatic *Nocturnes* are an atmospheric evocation of the river at London: the American, James McNeil Whistler.

But Monet's chief concern is with the visual phenomena of the real world rather than with art, and this view shows him responding to the challenge of depicting the actual sights of the bustling capital. The smoke of tugs and trains, from which earlier painters had turned in horror, becomes a source of atmospheric beauty. How much Monet was entranced by London is shown by the fact that he, like Pissarro also, returned in old age to paint the same sights, and to recapture the poetry of light perceived through a foggy shroud.

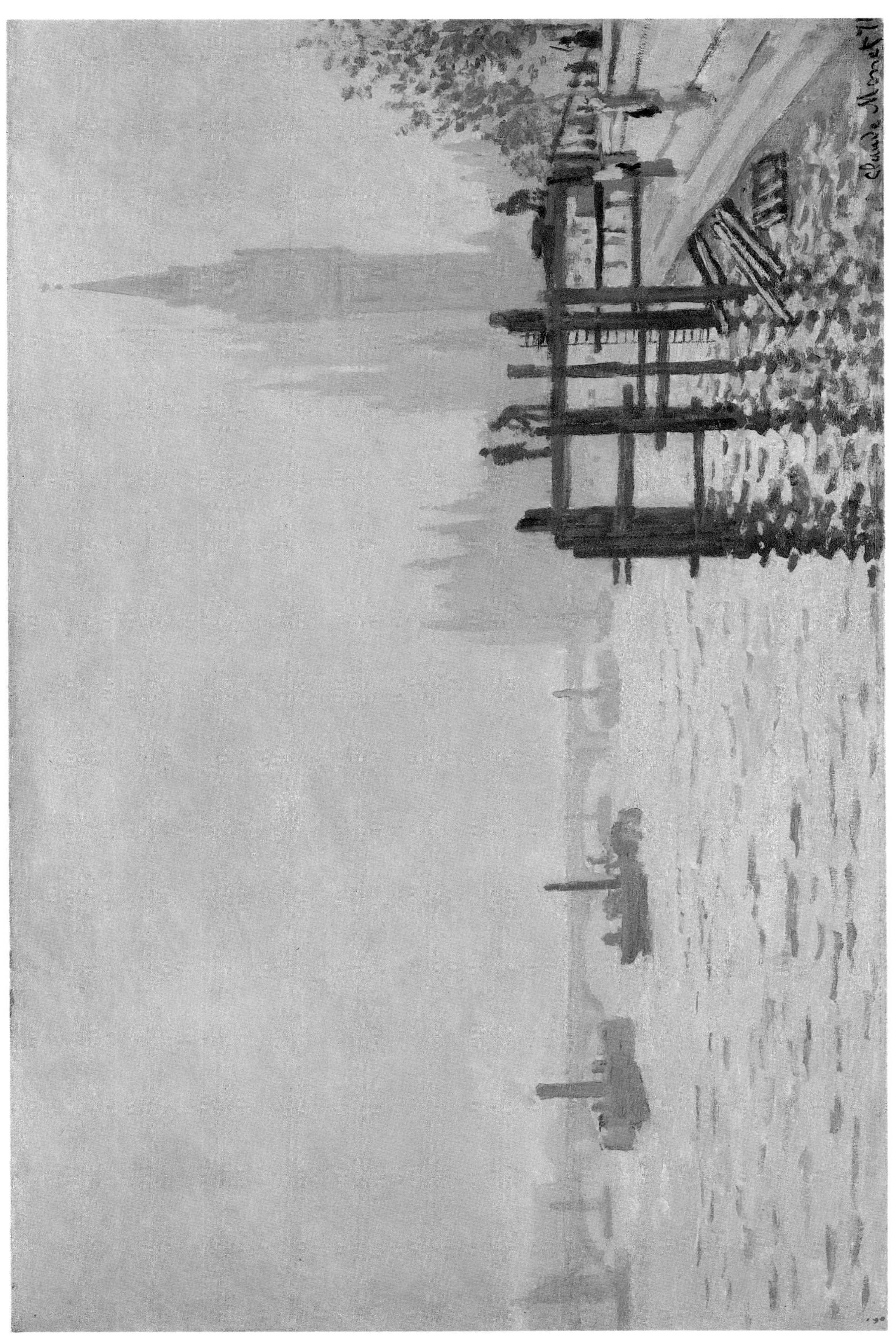

PLATE 24

Claude-Oscar Monet, 1840–1926

The Gare Saint-Lazare (No. 6479)

Signed: Claude Monet
Canvas, 53 × 72 cm.
Purchased 1982

At the fourth Impressionist exhibition in 1877, Monet exhibited a group of what were his most ambitious urban subjects to date: seven canvases of the Gare Saint-Lazare. Some, like this example, were painted from within the station, others, amid the maze of track at the approach to the station, afforded glimpses of the Pont de l'Europe and the surrounding apartment buildings. No one before had painted such views of the brand-new iron and glass stations, with their form and structure virtually obliterated by the dense atmosphere of smoke and steam, and his pictures came as a shock at the 1877 exhibition. In depicting the great steam locomotives that had so transformed the shape of the modern world, Monet drew no morals or lessons, and put before the public, without comment, something most people of taste believed to be irredeemably ugly. Renoir's friend Georges Rivière, in his review of the exhibition, struggled without success to find a way of describing these pictures, and found them 'enormously varied in spite of the monotony and aridity of the subject'. In his literary evocation of the station, he resorts to the comparison of a train with an 'impatient and temperamental beast', shaking its 'mane of smoke', while 'around the monster, men swarm on the tracks like pygmies at the feet of a giant.'

How much more discreet is Monet's canvas, which conveys all the rich atmosphere of the station without the fanciful exaggeration of Rivière's metaphors. For Monet the subject is as rich and as beautiful as the artist's penetrating vision of light, form and movement can make it. Above the tracks – the *grandes lignes* in the part of the station bordering on the rue d'Amsterdam – the roof of the shed rises to a great peak, imposing its structure on the composition of the painting. Below, in the cold light of the station, the great black hulks of the engines puff smoke and steam into the air, and hastily indicated railway men and passengers weave their way between the tracks. For all the predominance of iron and concrete the picture is far from lacking in colour: the roof is almost pure Prussian blue, and against the wintry sky steam and smoke make a harmony of blues, mauves and violets.

Monet's friend Renoir greatly admired the uncompromising originality of the Gare Saint-Lazare paintings, and also the artist's gall. He later recalled that by persuading the station-master that he was doing the railway an honour in desiring to work there, Monet had gained permission to paint in the station when and wherever he wished.

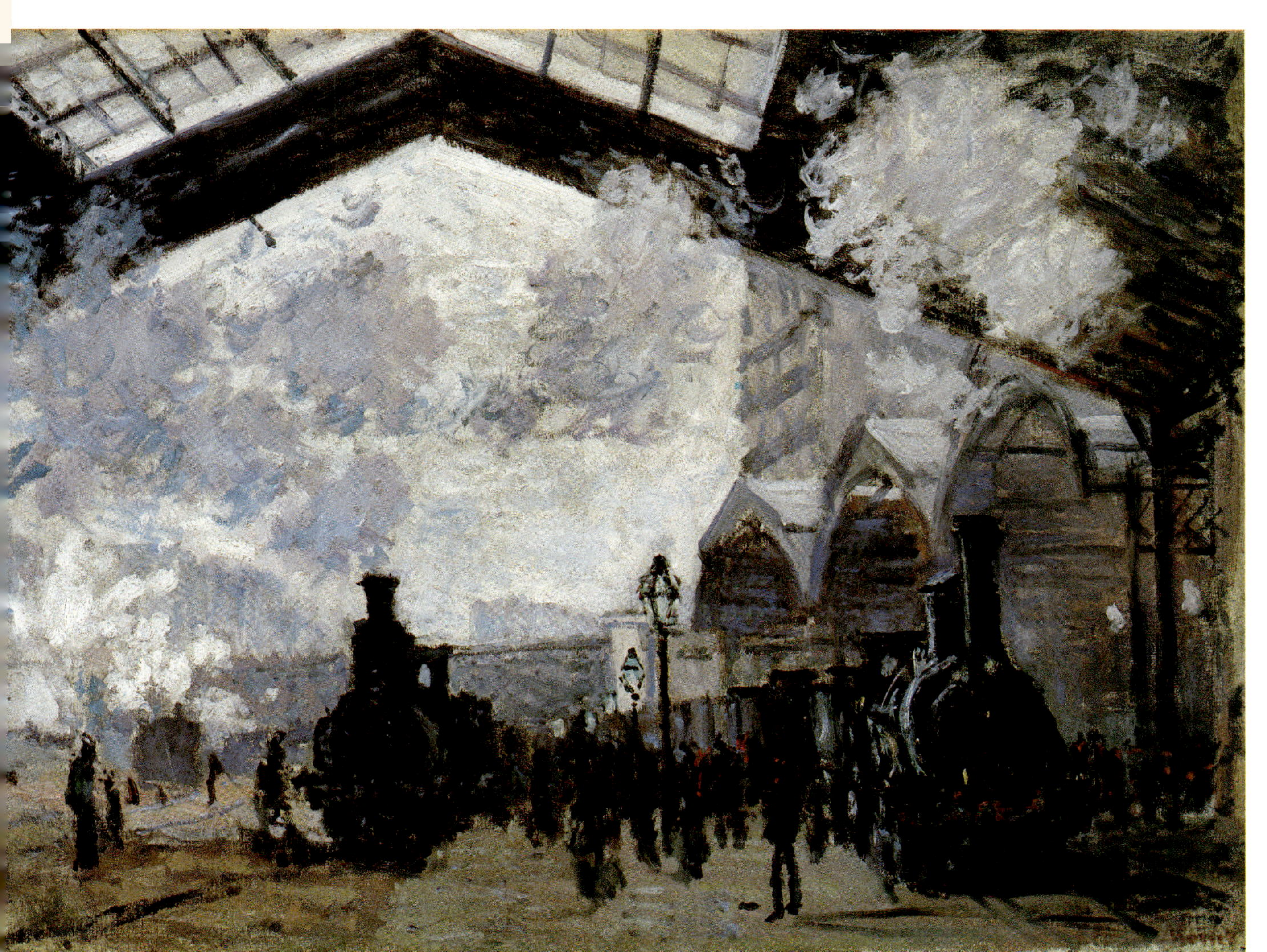

PLATE 25

Edouard Manet, 1832–1883

The Waitress (No. 3858)

Signed: Manet 78
Canvas, 97 × 77 cm.
Purchased, Courtauld Fund, 1924

The story behind this apparently straightforward painting of a scene in a Paris brasserie is unexpectedly complicated, and offers a fascinating insight into Manet's methods as an artist.

In August 1878 Manet is said to have started work on a large picture of the Brasserie de Reichshoffen which was apparently situated on either the boulevard de Rochechouart or the boulevard de Clichy. One of the waitresses came to pose for him, bringing with her a companion, the man seated in the foreground of the painting, smoking his pipe.

However, as he worked on the canvas, Manet radically altered his conception and cut the picture in two, completing the two halves separately. One part is this painting which Manet entitled *La Servante de Bocks*, the other, today in the Reinhart Collection, Winterthur, shows a man and two women seated at a café table and is called *Au Café*. Although Manet reworked each part they can still be seen to match, the table on the left of *The Waitress* joining with that in *Au Café*, and the shadows of the glasses and carafes continuing across the join. At the very edge of *The Waitress* at the far end of the table can even be seen part of the hand of the girl who sits on the other side of the table, in the Reinhart picture.

At some stage Manet also enlarged the picture at its right edge by adding an extra strip of canvas. The join is clearly visible running through the blue blouse of the seated man, roughly in line with the edge of the stage curtain above. This has the effect of bringing the waitress into the centre of the canvas and giving the revised composition balance. Having established this new picture Manet reworked the background, adding the stage, the dancer and the orchestra, which is painted in a much looser style than the foreground figures. He also painted a second, smaller version of *The Waitress*, which is today in the Louvre.

As the picture is in actual fact a fragment, so also is it conceived as a fragment of something more extensive. Like a snapshot, it extracts a single part from a scene of contemporary life. To each side the bustle of activity continues. The dancer gestures off left; the waitress glances off right; no one's eyes meet. Thus Manet hints at a truism of modern urban life, that even in the middle of a crowd, each person remains isolated.

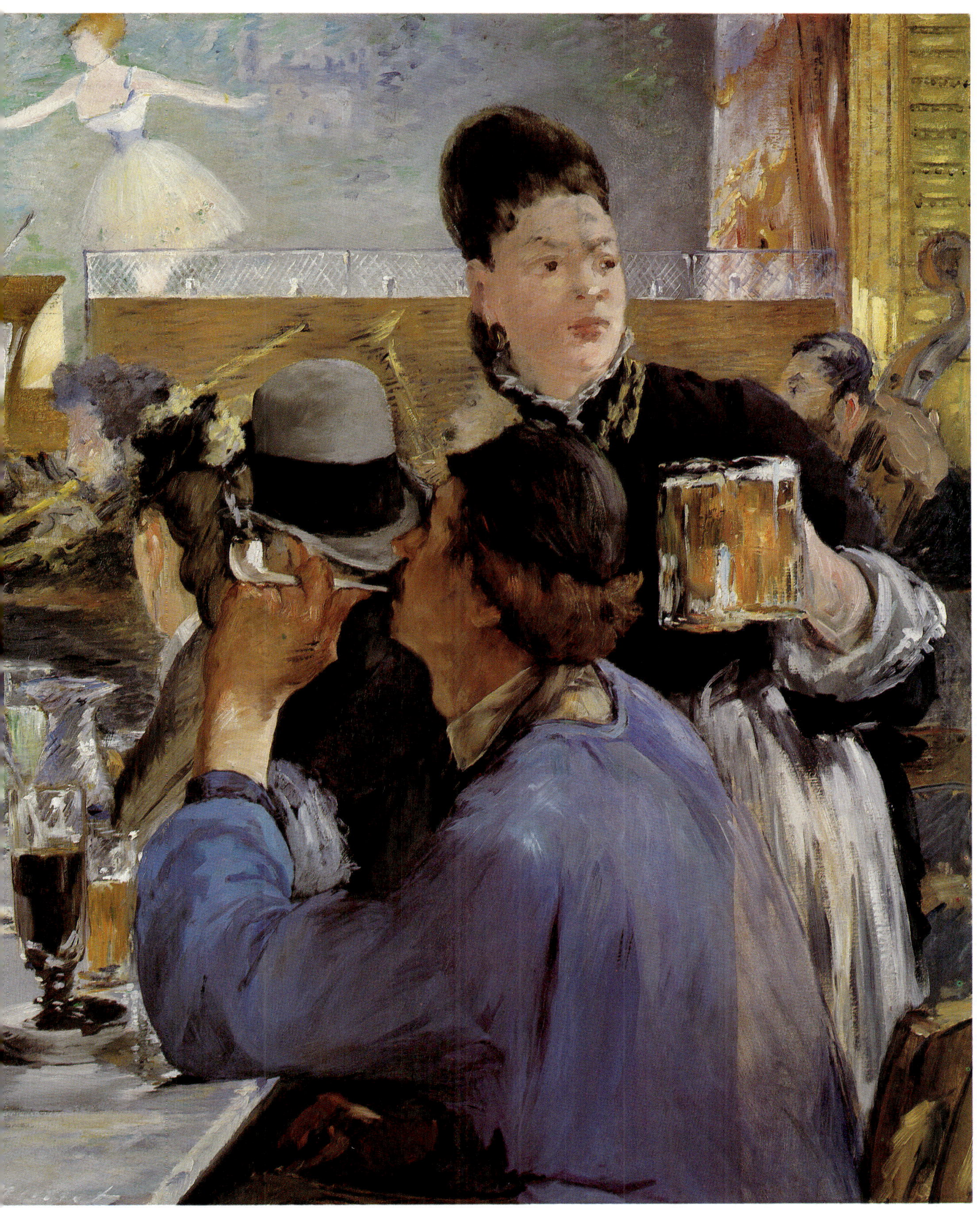

PLATE 26

Hilaire-Germain-Edgar Degas, 1834–1917

Beach Scene (No. 3247)

['Bains de Mer; Petite Fille peignée par sa Bonne']

Signed: Degas
Paper mounted on canvas, 47 × 82 cm.
Lane Bequest 1917

Beach scenes were particularly popular with the Impressionists and their forerunners among the artists of the previous generation. Following the example of Boudin and Courbet, Monet worked on the Channel coast (see Plate 21) and so also did Degas' friend Manet. But Degas' picture does not fall neatly into this Impressionist category in which light and the effects of weather usually constitute the chief interest. For a start Degas painted the central figure group in Paris, sitting on the floor of his studio, not in the open at all. And it is clear that his interest is focussed on this particular group of child and nurse rather than the scene as a whole. Laid on the yellow sand like paper cut-outs they have no relation to the panorama behind them, and seem not to belong to the same world as the doll-like figures dotted along the water's edge.

Degas was primarily a figure painter. Landscape generally forms no more than a background to seated jockeys or other figure groups. He belonged to the tradition of draughtsmen painters who used line to define anatomical form. He was an admirer of Ingres and the great Renaissance masters of line – Bronzino and before him Mantegna – and often drew inspiration from them. Although Degas' nursemaid and her charge belong to the contemporary world and are absorbed in an ordinary, even banal occupation, their pose relates closely to a pair of figures in an allegorical painting designed by Mantegna and executed by Lorenzo Costa, which Degas would have seen in the Louvre. For all its apparent naturalness, Degas' painting is thus a stage removed from the real world and takes on new meanings in relation to earlier art of which Degas was keenly aware. Maid and sleeping child recall groups of Delilah and the shorn Samson, or the Virgin and the infant Jesus whose sleeping posture was often intended as a pre-figurement of his death. In the light of such analogies how suggestive becomes the tender and silent combing of the little girl's hair.

Degas also had recourse to art of a more exotic kind. By taking a high viewpoint, he shows his figures and the distinctive forms of a bathing suit laid out to dry, an open parasol and a closed umbrella as coloured shapes against the flat background of the beach. With these familiar yet exquisitely placed objects, rendered without depth in the shadowless light, the picture has the same strange beauty as the woodblock prints of Japan.

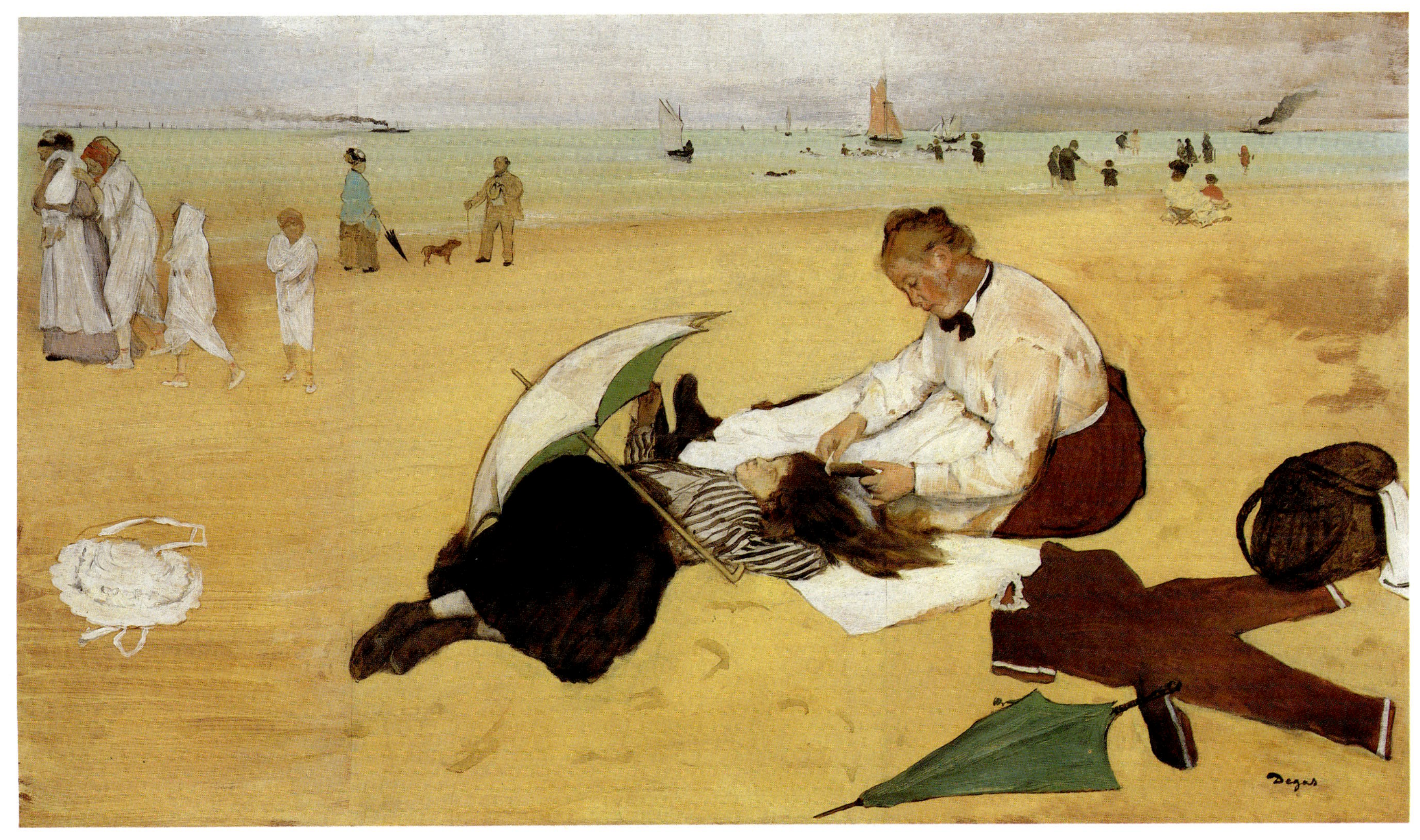
Degas

PLATE 27

Hilaire-Germain-Edgar Degas, 1834–1917

La La at the Cirque Fernando (No. 4121)

Signed: degas
Canvas, 117 × 77 cm.
Purchased, Courtauld Fund, 1925

Like his friend Manet, Degas was a thorough Parisian. He disliked travelling, had little time for the country, and took most of the subjects for his pictures from the sights around him. As Monet had done at the Gare Saint-Lazare, Degas sought out striking modern subjects hitherto untreated by painters. He preferred indoor scenes and liked to show professionals at work, particularly when, as entertainers, they were required to perform in an unusual way. He liked to concentrate on single figures, isolating them in arresting poses: a dancer pirouetting on a brilliantly illuminated stage, a singer gesturing to the audience of a café-concert, or, most remarkable of all, a circus performer suspended by her teeth from the vaults of a circus dome.

The circus Degas has painted is the Cirque Fernando on the corner of the boulevard Rochechouart and the rue des Martyrs, which was built in 1875; the performer, Miss La La, a mulatto acrobat who was noted for her feats of strength. Degas sketched at the circus in January 1879 and did a pastel study of Miss La La (now in the Tate Gallery) before embarking on the painting, which he exhibited in April at the fourth Impressionist exhibition.

The novelty of the circus, a gaudily decorated structure supported on iron girders, and Miss La La's act, must have had a double appeal for Degas. Always with an eye open for novel subjects, he must have quickly recognized the exciting pictorial possibilities offered by the figure of Miss La La suspended high in the dome of the circus. Degas offers us no glimpse of the audience or the ground. Instead we take the place of the spectator, gazing with neck strained at the daring feats taking place above us. To emphasize the soaring perspective, Degas has placed La La high up in the corner of the composition, at the outer limit of our field of vision. The angle of her outstretched arms and tilted legs takes up the line of the iron roof supports, which rise in a steep diagonal towards the peak of the circus dome. Slicing across the picture from top to bottom is a rope, taut with the weight of the suspended performer. To heighten the drama the gas lights shine upward from below, touching the stucco-work with highlights of gold, and illuminating the shimmering, air-borne circus star with an unnatural radiance.

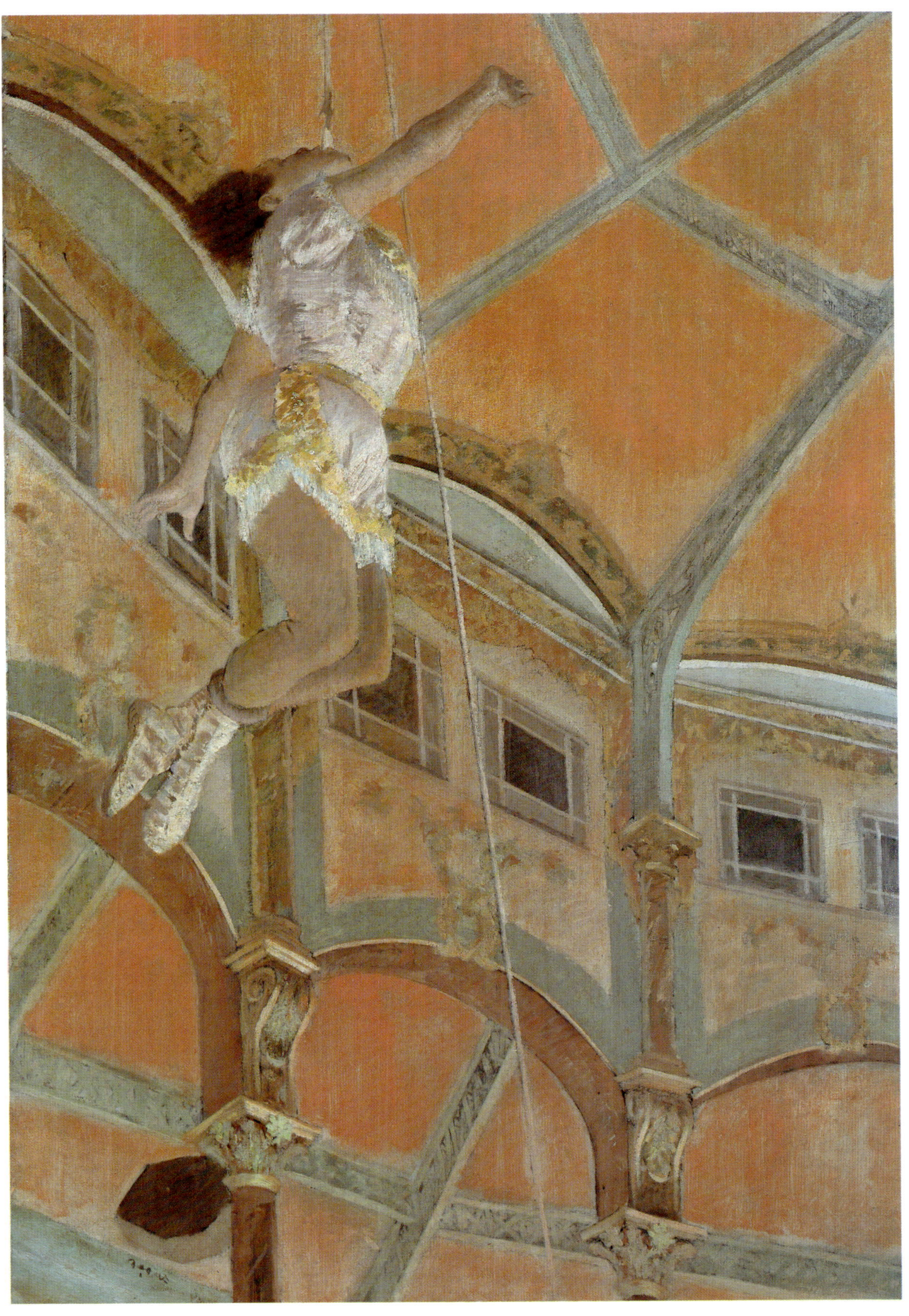

PLATE 28

Pierre-Auguste Renoir, 1841–1919

The Café-Concert (No. 3859)

['La Première Sortie']

Signed: Renoir

Canvas, 65 × 51 cm.

Purchased, Courtauld Fund, 1923

The exact subject of this picture, for all its popularity, is not easy to define. It was painted in about 1876 but no original title survives. In 1899 it was called *Le Café-Concert* and in 1918 the dealer Vollard referred to it as *Au Théâtre*. The popular title, *La Première Sortie* (the first outing), does not seem to have been applied before 1923 but it has had sufficient appeal to remain in general use.

Vollard's title, however, would seem to be the most appropriate. No one appears to be eating or drinking, and the well-dressed spectators are seated in tiers and boxes as at the theatre. The theatre, opera, and café-concert were favourite themes of the Impressionists and played an important role in Paris social life in the nineteenth century. An enormous number of ornately decorated theatres were built during the period, most notably Garnier's huge Opéra, and they provided painters with spectacles of modern life at its most colourful and glamorous. Degas often painted performances of ballet and opera, while Manet preferred to depict the more varied company that attended the café-concert. Renoir was especially fond of the glittering spectacle of the theatre and confessed to being far more engrossed by the audience than by the performance. He deplored the practice, introduced by Wagner, of dimming the lights in the auditorium.

Renoir's tastes were hardly sophisticated. He began his painting career as a decorator of porcelain, and he had simple likes and dislikes. He preferred Offenbach to Wagner and he was attracted above all by the innocent charm of pretty young girls. In this painting he shows a young girl, bouquet of flowers in hand, gazing with rapt attention at the stage. Her naive enthusiasm is vividly contrasted with the nonchalance of the men and women whom we glimpse beyond, glancing around them, and turning to one another with the latest gossip. Renoir shares the other Impressionists' interest in atmosphere and light, and this picture is partly concerned with the evocation of mood through the use of indistinct forms and merging colours. But perhaps more than any of his fellow Impressionists, he is concerned with his subject and likes to hint at the thoughts and emotions that animate his models. No doubt the modern title *La Première Sortie* has gained such wide currency because, in suggesting an anecdotal flavour, it responds to the mood of the painting itself and the artist's affectionate interest in his innocent young theatre-goer.

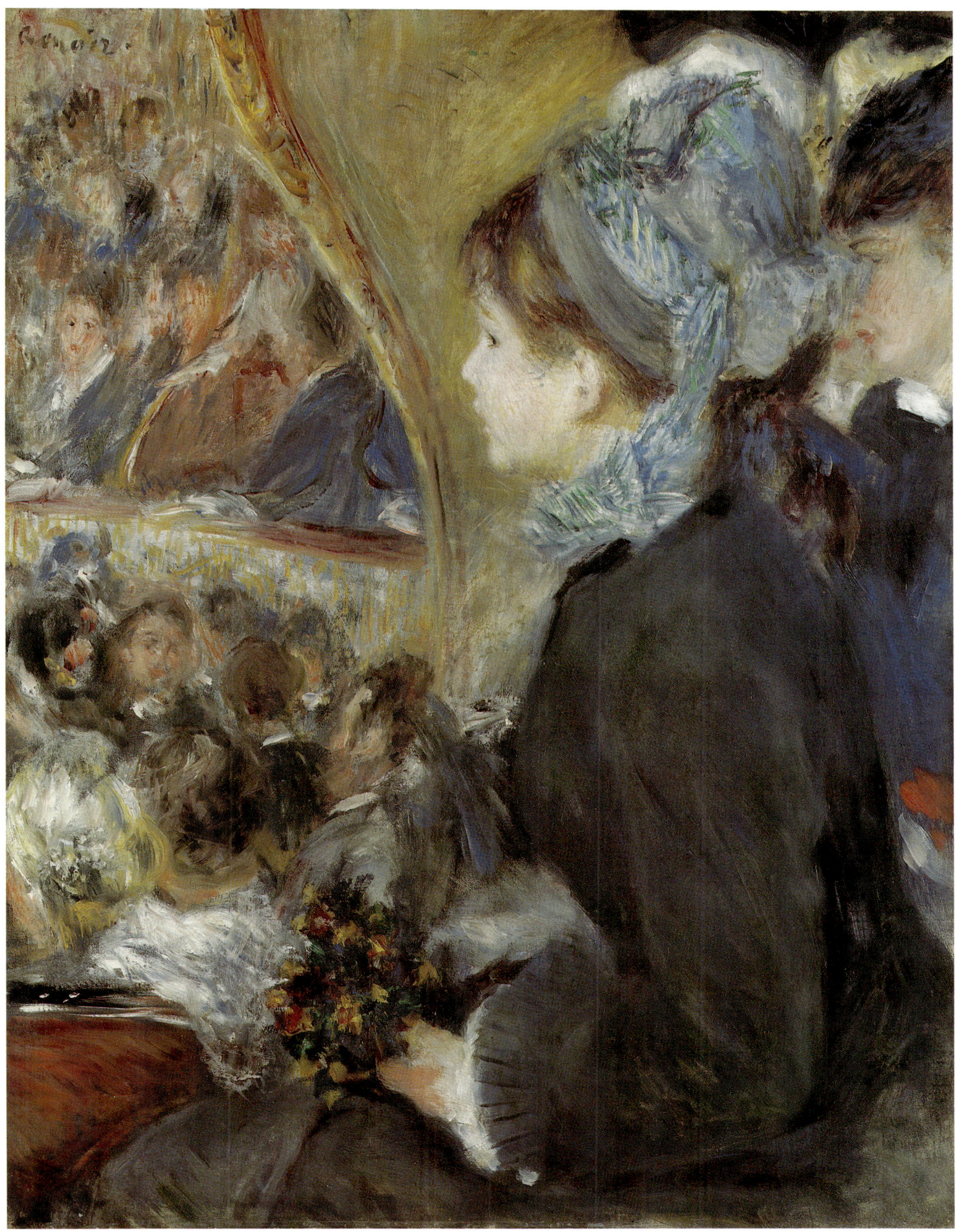
Renoir.

PLATE 29

Pierre-Auguste Renoir, 1841–1915

The Seine at Asnières (No. 6478)

['La Yole']

Signed: Renoir
Canvas, 71 × 92 cm.
Purchased 1982

This brilliantly colourful river-scene epitomizes much of what is so popular in Impressionist painting: a sun-drenched view, people enjoying themselves by the river, and intensely luminous paint freely applied with consummate ease.

By the time Renoir painted this picture about ten years had elapsed since he worked with Monet at La Grenouillère (see Plate 19) and the river had become a favourite subject with the Impressionists. For Monet the interest of such scenes lay above all in the way the movement of the water created broken images of reflected light; it suggested to him how a broken surface texture of colour might recapture the brilliance of light in painting. While Renoir was influenced by Monet's discoveries, he was more enthralled by the life of the river. Like so many of his fellow Parisians, Renoir frequented those resorts on the Seine just to the north-west of Paris, where the city began to give way to countryside. There, on Sundays, would come parties of young people from the crowded suburbs to enjoy the pleasures of boating, bathing and dining at the river-side cafés.

Bougival, Chatou, Argenteuil and La Grenouillère have all been made famous by Impressionist painting. At Asnières, where Renoir painted this view, Seurat, Van Gogh and Emile Bernard also painted. The railway bridge on the right of the picture in fact appears in the background of Seurat's large canvas, *Bathers, Asnières* (plate 31). And the train which Renoir has shown approaching the bridge, puffing white smoke, is *en route* for the Gare Saint-Lazare which Monet had made the subject of a series of paintings only two years or so previously (see Plate 24).

Renoir is not a theorizing artist or a painter of ideas. His picture is a straightforward but nonetheless atmospheric description of a particular place at a given time. Beyond the further bank, close to the railway line, stands a substantial modern villa, characteristic of the new suburbs. Along the river's edge are dotted boats, and occasional figures, and in the foreground two women (or is it perhaps a man rowed by a woman?) glide by in a skiff. Yet in spite of the modest subject matter, how skilfully Renoir evokes the mood of a summer's day, with the incandescent sunlight glowing on walls and shimmering on the water. The effect of the orange boat reflected in the ultramarine water is unforgettable.

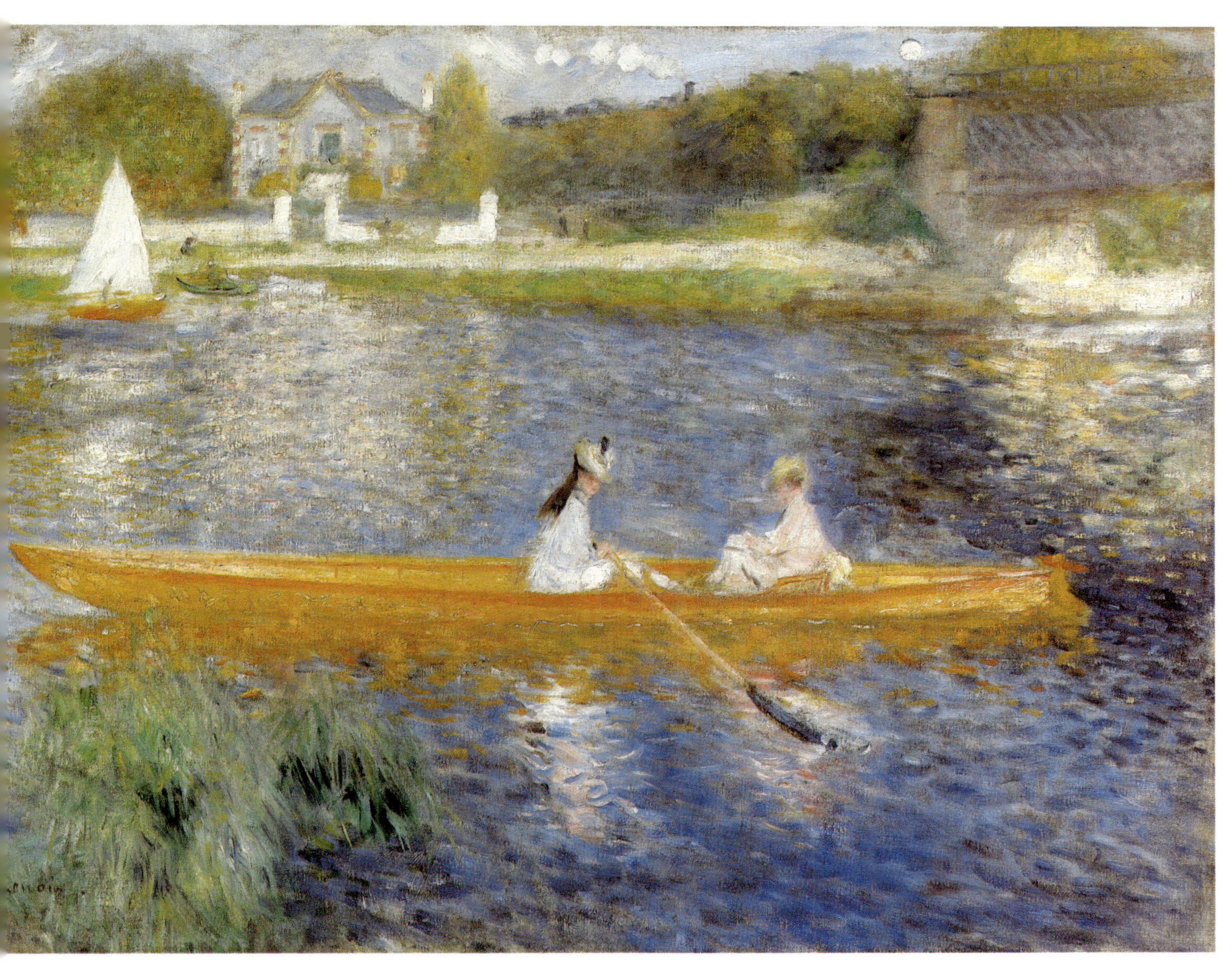

PLATE 30

Pierre-Auguste Renoir, 1841–1919

The Umbrellas (No. 3268)

Signed: Renoir
Canvas, 180 × 115 cm.
Lane Bequest 1917

Since the success of the portrait of *Madame Charpentier and her Children* at the Salon of 1879 Renoir had enjoyed a healthy demand for his work, and the income from his commissions permitted him for the first time in his life to travel, to Italy and Algiers in 1881 and again to Algiers in 1882.

Ironically, however, the very moment that success was his, he became plagued by doubt and dissatisfaction. 'I had gone to the end of Impressionism,' he later recalled, 'and I was reaching the conclusion that I didn't know how either to paint or to draw. In a word, I was at a dead end.' The crisis coincided with a critical illness. Early in 1882, after several months travelling through southern Italy and Sicily, he returned by sea to Marseilles and joined Cézanne at l'Estaque where he caught pneumonia. Cézanne and his mother nursed the painter back to health, but the letters he wrote during his illness show that his spirits were at a very low ebb.

Renoir's artistic re-emergence was a slow and painful process. He felt that in turning to nature alone as his guide he had forsaken the time-hallowed principles of art. He had been deeply struck by the frescoes of Raphael in the Vatican and by the ancient Roman wall-paintings in the museum at Naples, and hoped to achieve an equivalent classicism of his own, with something of the same purity of line and strength of form.

It is against this background that *The Umbrellas* should be seen, since it was painted over a period of years during the first half of the 1880s and shows him struggling to master a new manner. It is in fact painted in two different techniques: the woman and children on the right in the soft merging colours of his Impressionist years, the girl on the left and the umbrellas in a new linear style with subdued colour and clearly defined forms, showing the lessons of Raphael and Herculaneum. The different fashions of the women's clothes suggest that a considerable period, perhaps as much as five years, elapsed before he completed the picture in about 1886.

In the later parts of the picture, however, another influence is also apparent. Staying with Cézanne at Aix, Renoir had been greatly impressed by his friend's recent work, which few had seen, and in various parts of *The Umbrellas*, particularly the trees at the top and the umbrellas themselves, he adopted Cézanne's technique of parallel hatchings of paint to represent planes. Thus the lessons of Raphael and Cézanne and the South came together in his mind as the pursuit of classical economy in the rendition of form. 'I am in the process of learning a lot,' he wrote from Aix. 'While warming myself and observing a great deal, I shall, I believe, have acquired the simplicity and grandeur of the ancient painters.'

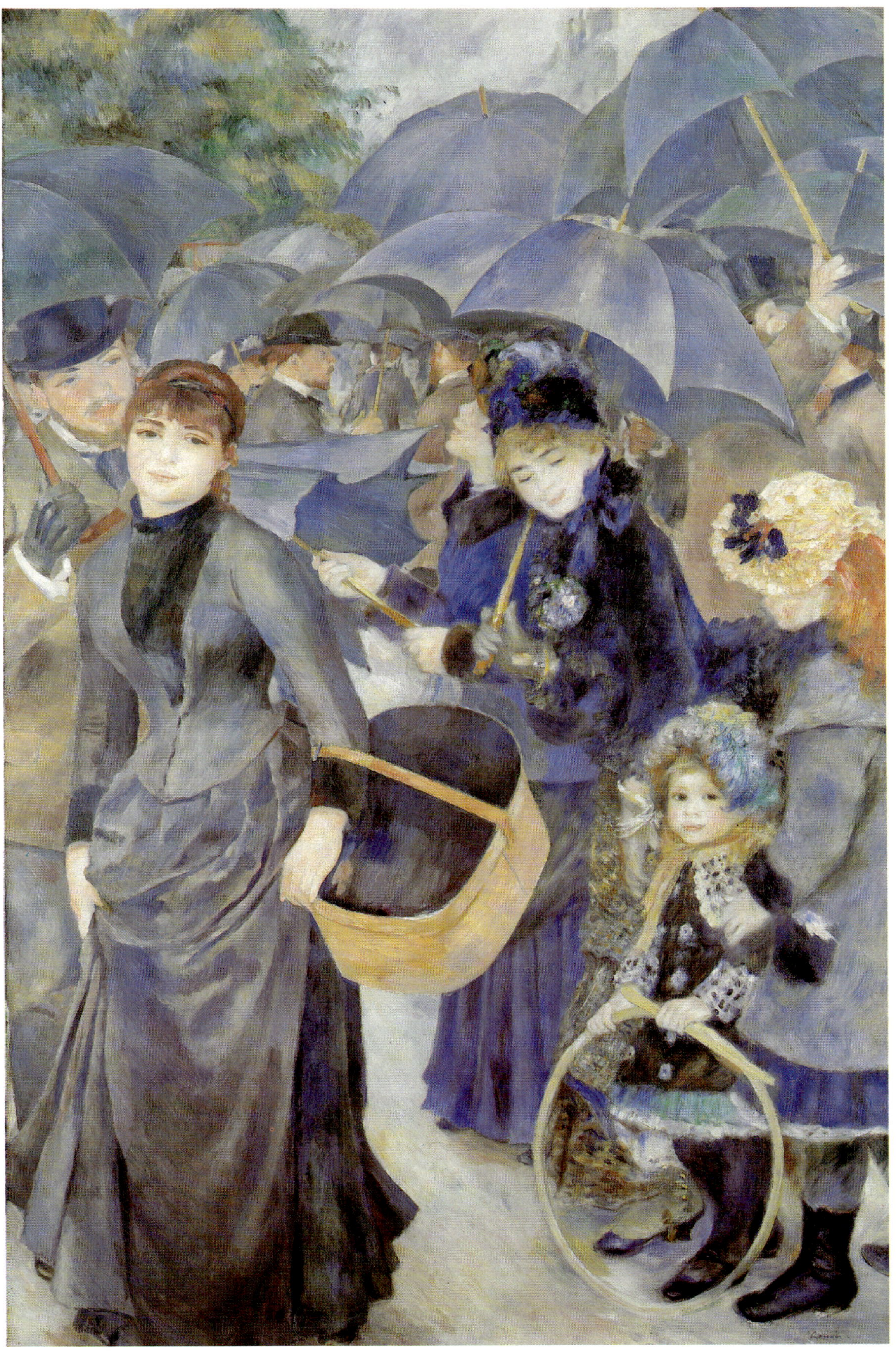

PLATE 31

Georges-Pierre Seurat, 1859–1891

Bathers, Asnières (No. 3908)

Signed: Seurat

Canvas, 201 × 301 cm.

Purchased, Courtauld Fund, 1924

Seurat's huge canvas of Bathers represents a scene on the Seine near Asnières very close to that depicted by Renoir in '*La Yole*' (Plate 29): the railway bridge to the right of Renoir's painting is the same as that in the background of Seurat's. A generation younger than the Impressionists, Seurat was nevertheless attracted to similar subjects, but his manner of treating them is quite different.

Bathers, Asnières is Seurat's first major composition, and was painted when he was not yet twenty-five. He submitted it to the Salon of 1884 but it was rejected and he subsequently exhibited it at the newly formed Salon des Artistes Indépendants. The painting is much larger than the average Impressionist canvas; and was carefully executed in the studio, not out of doors in one or two sessions. Little about it is spontaneous; it is the result of long study. A whole series of oil sketches of the site, and numerous conté crayon drawings of the figures prepared the way for the final composition. In comparison with the atmospheric landscapes of Monet and Renoir, the result may seem stilted. There is little suggestion of movement. The figures are as immobile as statues. Even the boats on the river seem halted in their progress. And no fleeting effects of light are caught by an agile brush. The sky is clear, and the dazzling midday sunlight serves rather to define forms and cast them in stillness. The reflections in the water and the shadows are as fixed as the figures. No breeze stirs the trees; they are as solidly sculpted as the bridge and the factories with their ranks of chimneys.

In an attempt to create something as monumental and timeless as the sculptures of the ancients, and the paintings of Piero della Francesca and Poussin which he had studied as a pupil at the Ecole des Beaux-Arts, Seurat rejected the spontaneity of the Impressionists and moulded his composition in simplified blocks of light and shade. His bathers are featureless and impassive, and like the figures in a frieze are shown in profile. And although he had not yet arrived at the systematic application of paint in dots of pure colour known as *divisionisme* which he later adopted, Seurat has applied his paint in a uniform hatchwork of blended colours, which, without describing texture, binds the surface in a tightly integrated pictorial whole.

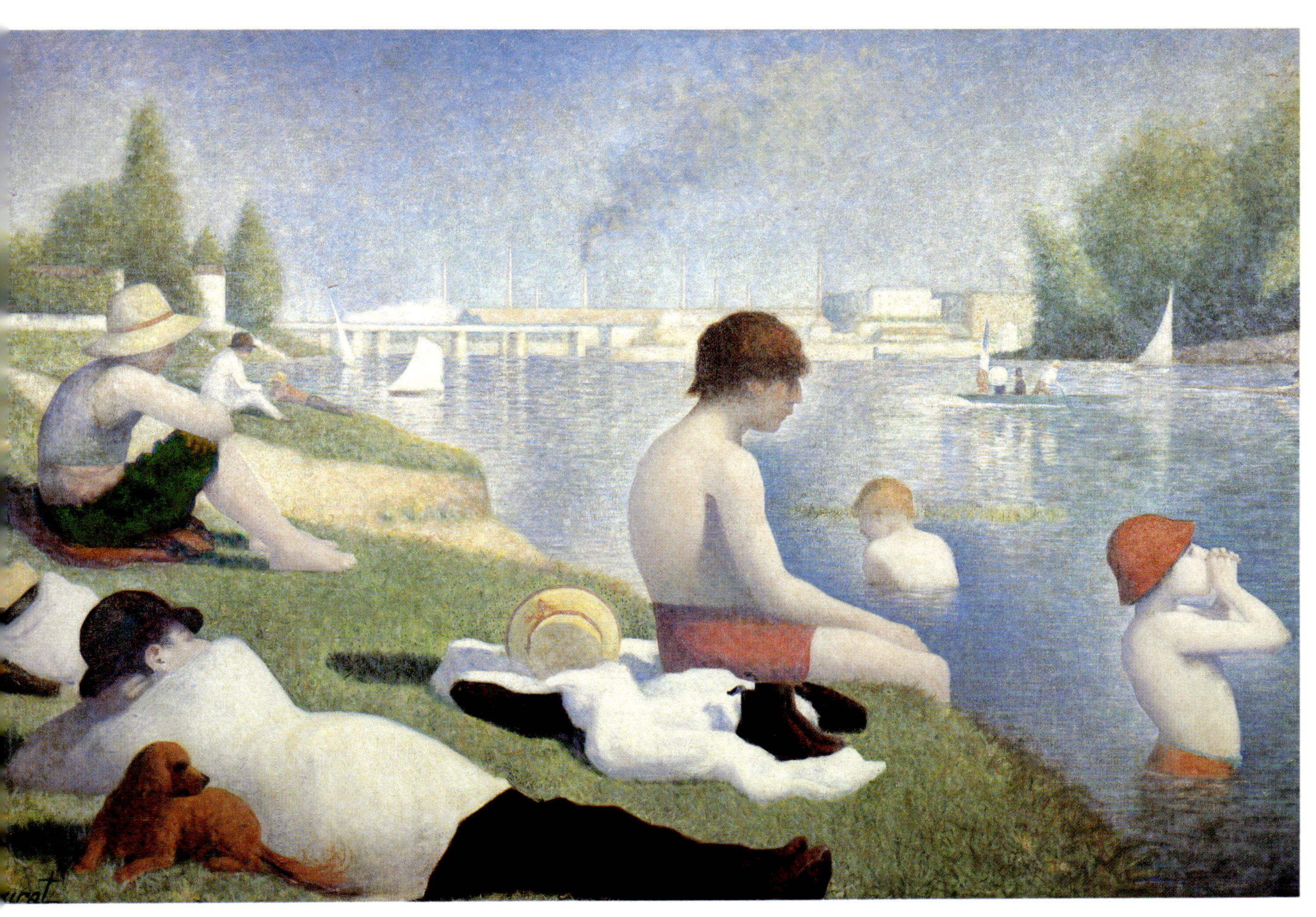

PLATE 32

Hilaire-Germain-Edgar Degas, 1834–1917

Hélène Rouart in her Father's Study (No. 6469)

Stamped: Degas
Canvas, 161 × 120 cm.
Purchased 1981

A young woman in a plain high-necked dress stands alone in a study, gently resting her hands on the back of an over-sized chair. To one side is a paper-strewn table and a glass case containing Egyptian wood statues, the nearest, a *Ushabti*, or funerary figurine, of the Middle Kingdom. High on the wall behind is a Chinese silk hanging of the Ch'ing Dynasty, and on the right are two pictures, an early oil study by Corot of *The Bay of Naples and the Castello dell'Ovo* and a drawing by Millet of a seated peasant.

The woman is Hélène Rouart, the only daughter of Degas' life-long friend Henri Rouart (1833–1912), who himself painted and exhibited at seven of the eight Impressionist group shows. Degas had painted her as a girl on her father's knee in about 1877 and this later portrait was completed in 1886 when Hélène was apparently eighteen. The picture is broad in execution and reveals various changes, particularly in the red and blue lines that redefine the contours of Hélène's figure. But it is not necessarily unfinished. It does not seem to have been a commission, and considering his strong links with the Rouart family, Degas could have painted it for himself. Degas had first intended to paint the entire Rouart family, and then planned a painting of Hélène with her mother. Two pastels and a drawing show Hélène standing wrapped in a shawl, like a statue herself, admiring a Tanagra figurine with her mother. Probably on account of Madame Rouart's ill-health, Degas eventually painted Hélène alone in her father's study in the family house on the rue de Lisbonne.

As on other occasions Degas has painted a portrait in which the objects surrounding the sitter help to define her personality. Above all he hints at strong ties between father and daughter, since the objects surrounding Hélène belong in fact to Henri Rouart, who was a notable collector. His presence is evoked by the objects from his collection and also by the empty seat on which Hélène rests her hands. Hélène is presented as someone nurtured in a cultivated home but, like the statue in the glass case, she seems hemmed in by her environment, a sensitive girl on the verge of womanhood over-protected by a too-fond father. With sad eyes and a curious half-smile, she wistfully gazes out from behind his chair.

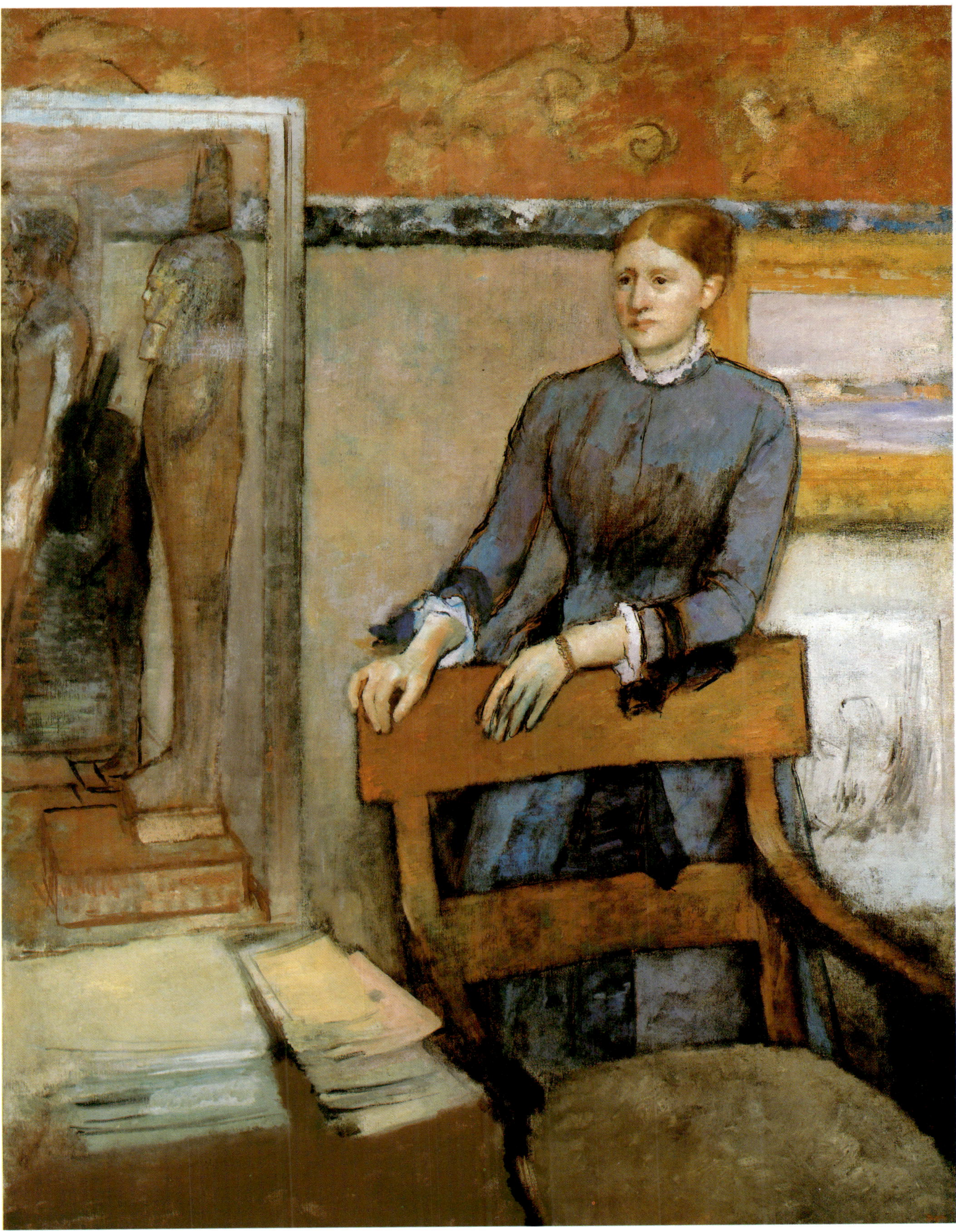

PLATE 33

Paul Cézanne, 1839–1906

Self-Portrait (No. 4135)

Canvas, 33.6 × 26 cm.
Purchased, Courtauld Fund, 1925

It is often forgotten that until 1877 Cézanne exhibited with the Impressionists. He was older in fact than Monet, Renoir and Sisley. But the 1860s and 70s were apprentice years for him, and he had to wait longer to achieve mastery and recognition. At the Impressionist exhibitions his works were the constant butt of abuse and ribaldry, and in 1877 he left Paris to lead a hermit-like existence at the Jas de Bouffan near Aix, his family home in the south of France.

With his black hair, swarthy complexion, piercing eyes and rough provincial accent, Cézanne must have seemed like a savage in Paris. Not surprisingly it was with Pissarro and Renoir, the most ingenuous of the Impressionist group, that he enjoyed the happiest relations. With others he was argumentative and given to emotional outbursts. His morbid sensitivity and abrasiveness were exacerbated by the frustration he experienced as an artist. Lacking the manual dexterity of Monet and Renoir, Cézanne had to struggle to give shape to his strong sensations. His earliest pictures are coarsely worked paintings of imaginary subjects in which the sombre colouring is matched by a darkness of theme – scenes of violence, suffering and eroticism.

Little of this is evident in this portrait that Cézanne painted of himself in about 1880 when he was forty-one. The bald-headed painter stares out of the canvas with a steady, impenetrable gaze, betraying no trace of passion. Under the tutorship of Pissarro, Cézanne had adopted a more objective approach, painting directly from nature, and harnessed his intense artistic sensibilities through the orderly analysis of structure and tonal values. By dint of rigorous self-control, Cézanne observes himself in this picture without emotion, and directs his attention at the geometry of forms, the way the dome of his head reacts with the diamond pattern of the wallpaper, which is in turn echoed by the silhouetted lapel of his jacket. 'See in nature the sphere, the cylinder, the cone,' Cézanne later advised his young disciples. By just such a discipline, Cézanne here achieves self-detachment, and a pictorial coherence which is orderly, lucid and harmonious.

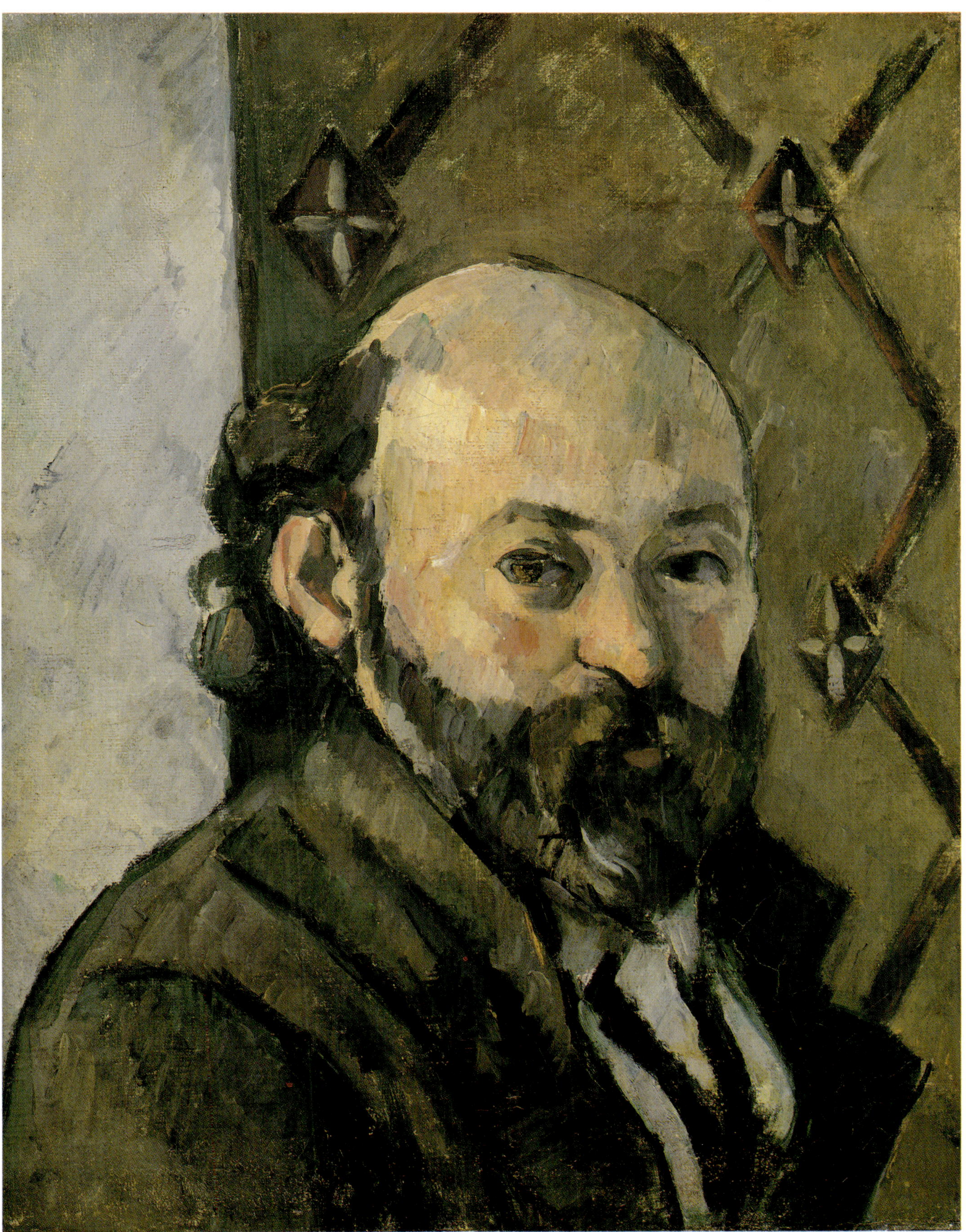

PLATE 34

Paul Cézanne, 1839–1906

Mountains in Provence (No. 4136)

Canvas, 63 × 79 cm.
Purchased, Courtauld Fund, 1926

Although a friend of Renoir and Monet, and a participant in the early Impressionist exhibitions, Cézanne lacked the natural facility to capture, as Monet did, fleeting atmospheric effects, and strove towards an alternative means of representing nature. After 1877 he ceased to exhibit with the Impressionists, and spent most of his time in the south, at l'Estaque or at his family home near Aix. 'Motifs can be found here which would require three or four months' work, and that is possible because the vegetation doesn't change,' he wrote to his friend and patron Victor Chocquet. 'It is composed of olive and pine trees which always preserve their foliage. The sun is so terrific that it seems to me as if the objects were silhouetted not only in black and white, but in blue, red, brown and violet.'

In pictures of the mountainous Provençal landscape, such as this one painted in about 1886, Cézanne evolved an approach that subordinated the changing effects of light and atmosphere to underlying structure. The fierce sunlight serves to throw into relief the rocky cliffs, which are immutable in their rugged massiveness. Beyond rises a mountain, stripped of all surface features except odd boundaries of fields which are like scratches engraved on the surface of a broad earthen dome.

Throughout the picture, even in the scant vegetation that grows across the cliffs, Cézanne uses a technique of parallel hatchings of paint which serve to model form and, as colour accents across the surface, link part to part in a logical spatial relationship. This carefully modulated colour, which Cézanne only achieved after long and laborious effort, also establishes an overall pictorial harmony. The result is not so much an imitation of nature, such as a photograph would provide, as an interpretation of nature as experienced by the artist. Art, Cézanne claimed, constituted for him 'a harmony running parallel to nature', and the juxtaposition of tones and the texture of hatchings, which he used in preference to traditional illusionistic devices, were his means of creating such a harmony.

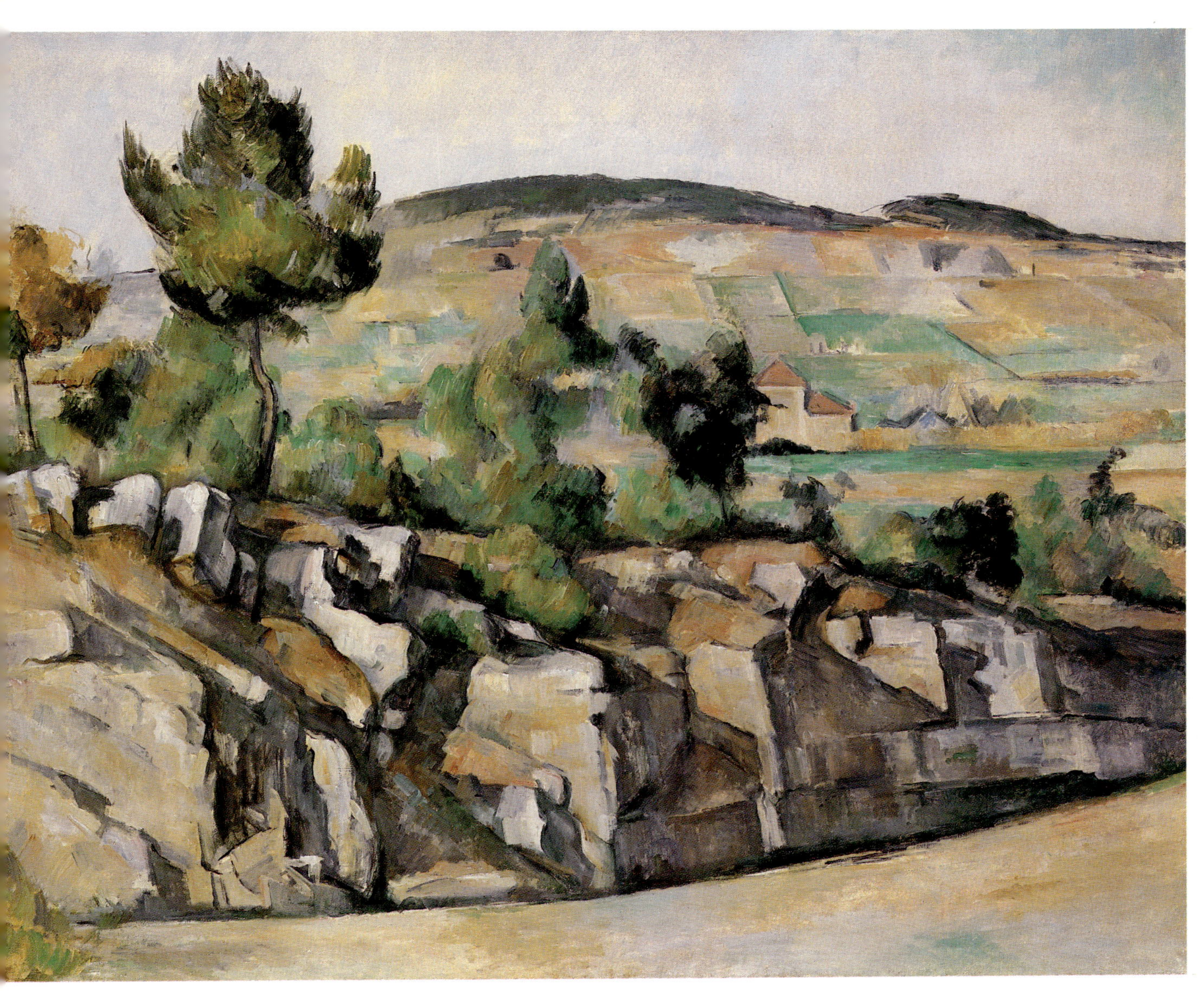

PLATE 35

Vincent Van Gogh, 1853–1890

Sunflowers (No. 3863)

Signed: Vincent
Canvas, 92 × 73 cm.
Purchased, Courtauld Fund, 1924

It is difficult to think of Van Gogh's pictures of sunflowers as flower paintings at all. The fat, globed seed-heads, some still fringed with bedraggled petals, protrude from the vase on long tubular stems, writhing and twisting in contortions that seem painful. The colour is almost monochromatic, the heavy ochres and yellows relieved only by a sickly green and the blue contours round the vase, across the background, and spelling out the artist's name.

This extraordinary revolution in painting was achieved by a poor Dutchman working alone in provincial France. Within two brief years in Paris, where he arrived in 1886 at the encouragement of his brother Theo, Van Gogh had absorbed the lessons of the Impressionists. He renounced the dark colours of his earlier years in Holland for their brilliant palette and for a short time experimented with a pointillist technique derived from Seurat. But it was at Arles, where he moved early in 1888 and became intoxicated with the dazzling sunlight, that Van Gogh established his own style. The local countryside, the citizens of Arles and the meagre furnishings of his house form his subjects, but they are transformed into vitally expressive images through the medium of brilliantly coloured, thickly impastoed paint.

In the late summer of 1888 Van Gogh wrote to his brother, 'I am thinking of decorating my studio with half a dozen pictures of sunflowers, a decoration in which the raw or broken chrome yellows will blaze forth on various backgrounds – blue, from the palest malachite green to royal blue.' Later he wrote again, perhaps in reference to this particular picture, of a painting showing 'a bunch of fourteen flowers against a yellow background'. He also spoke of decorating the guest room which he was preparing for Gauguin 'in the Japanese style', with six large canvases of sunflowers. Gauguin arrived in Arles late in October and during the troubled two months he spent with Van Gogh, painted him at work on a picture of sunflowers.

The subject clearly had an obsessive attraction for Van Gogh. He returned to it again early in 1889, when his fits of insanity had led to him being confined in the hospital at Arles, and produced variants of the pictures he had painted the previous autumn. In this example, painted in 1888, the thickly worked flower heads silhouetted against the luminous yellow ground fill the canvas. Like a symbol of harvest and the scorching heat of the south, it forms an overwhelmingly dense field of gold.

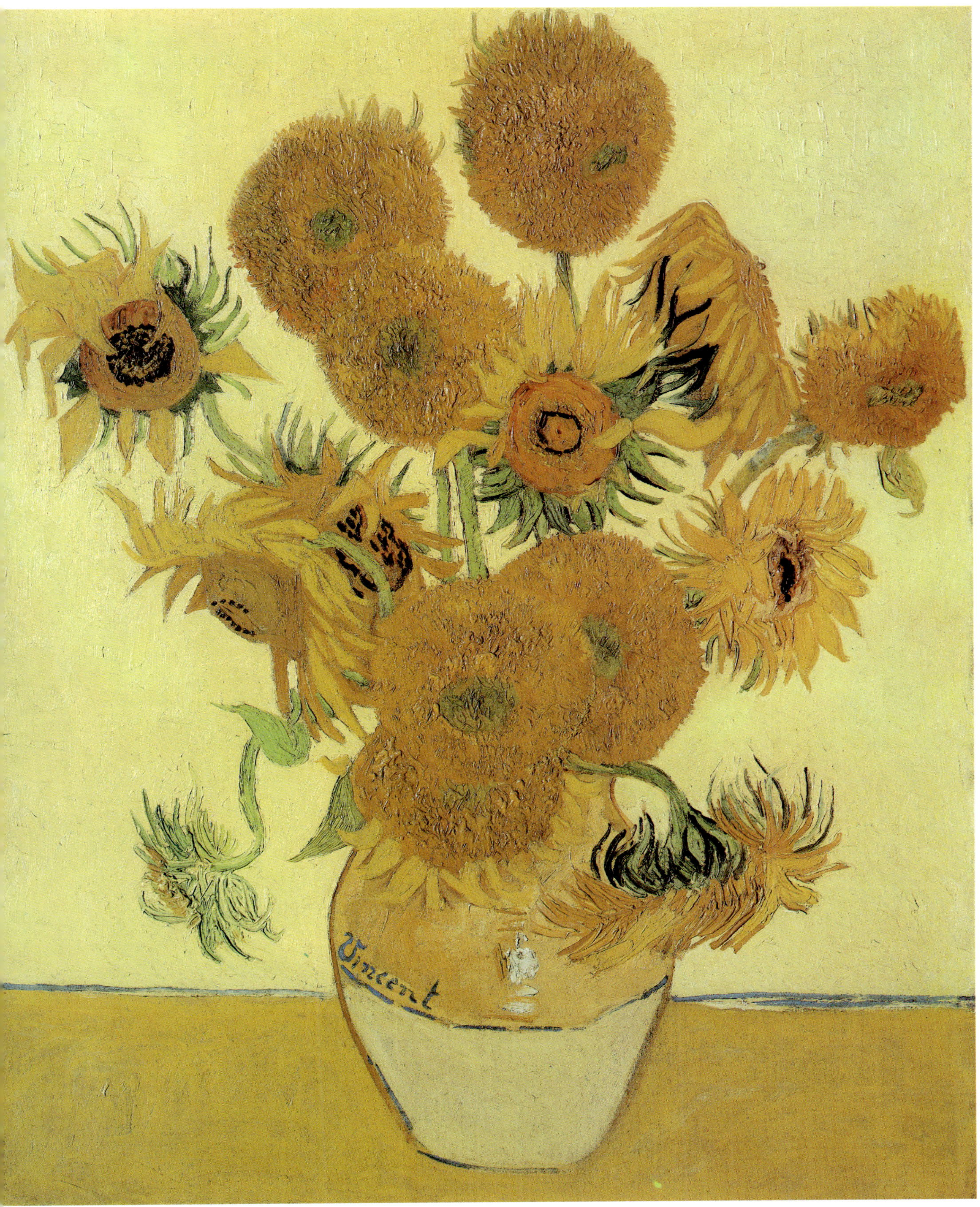
Vincent

PLATE 36

Vincent Van Gogh, 1853–1890

The Chair and the Pipe (No. 3862)

Signed: Vincent

Canvas, 92 × 73 cm.

Purchased, Courtauld Fund, 1924

This painting was begun late in 1888 while Gauguin was staying with Van Gogh at Arles but not completed until early in 1889. The intervening events are well-known. On December 23rd Van Gogh, in a fit of insanity, threatened Gauguin with an open razor, and subsequently mutilated himself, cutting off part of his left ear. Gauguin left Arles without seeing his friend again, and Van Gogh was interned in the local hospital.

In spite of Van Gogh's deep admiration for him, Gauguin never regarded Van Gogh highly as a painter and had little affection for him. As both men were passionate and volatile it is hardly surprising that their brief association at Arles should have ended in violence. Even as he made the arrangements for Gauguin's arrival, Van Gogh had confessed, 'if we each live alone it means living like madmen or criminals.' Ironically, living together only hastened the deterioration of Van Gogh's mental and physical state.

In the light of these circumstances, *The Chair and the Pipe* takes on a particular poignancy. The chair is the artist's, and was painted as a pair to a picture of Gauguin's armchair which Van Gogh also painted in December 1888 (and which is today in the Rijksmuseum Vincent Van Gogh, Amsterdam). 'I can at all events tell you that the last two studies are odd enough,' Van Gogh wrote to his brother, 'canvases of 30, a wooden rush-bottom chair all yellow on red tiles against a wall (daytime). Then Gauguin's armchair, red and green night effect, walls and floor red and green again, on the seat two novels and a candle.'

The 'odd' studies make a curious pair of opposites. Gauguin's chair, seen in candlelight, is an elaborate curved-back affair with arms; Van Gogh's is a simple peasant's chair. The one turned to the left, the other to the right, they thus seem to represent the tragic confrontation of the artists themselves, their contrasting forms mirroring the characters of the artists: Gauguin, a person of supreme confidence and subtle intelligence, and Van Gogh, a man of complete honesty, whose strength of feeling was to destroy him.

The Chair and the Pipe owes its strength to the element of personal feeling with which it is imbued. The stocky yellow chair, the pipe and paper of tobacco, the box of sprouting onions inscribed with Van Gogh's name, and even the door with its prominent hinge, all take on a reality which, as seen and felt through the artist's eyes, is larger than life. The physical immediacy of the artist's vision is emphasized by the coarse canvas and thickly worked paint, its intensity by the bright yellow of the chair with its vivid mauve outlines.

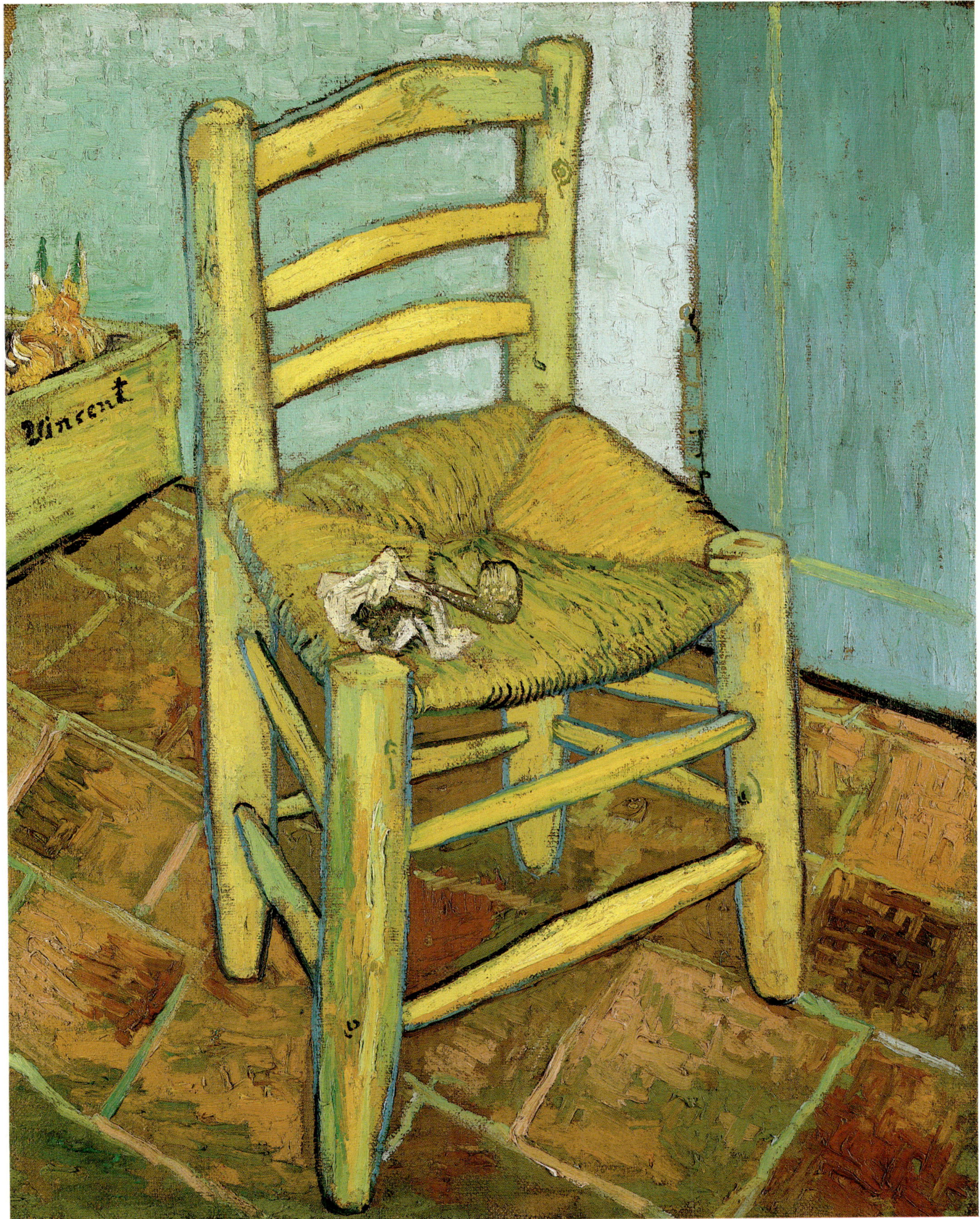
Vincent

PLATE 37

Vincent Van Gogh, 1853–1890

A Cornfield with Cypresses (No. 3861)

Canvas, 72 × 91 cm.
Purchased, Courtauld Fund, 1923

'The Cypresses are always occupying my thoughts,' wrote Van Gogh in June 1889. 'I would like to make something of them like the canvases of the sunflowers, because it astonishes me that they have not yet been done as I see them. It is as beautiful in line and proportion as an Egyptian obelisk. And the green has a quality of such distinction. It is a splash of black in a sunny landscape.'

A Cornfield with Cypresses is one of several canvases with cypresses that Van Gogh painted in the asylum at Saint-Rémy where he was a patient for a year from May 1889. When he was confined to his room he worked at his own interpretations of paintings by Rembrandt, Millet, Delacroix and Doré, prints of which his brother Theo had sent him. When well enough to go outside he painted the grounds of the old hospital and the surrounding countryside. Several canvases, dating from the late summer of 1889, show cornfields with mountains beyond, and in his letters Van Gogh spoke of painting a group of cypresses in the corner of a wheatfield during a summer *mistral*. Here the wind fills everything with a turbulent movement. The same writhing rhythms animate sky, hills and trees. As Van Gogh pointed out, no one had painted cypresses or indeed other forms of nature in such a way before. Nonetheless it is interesting to note that Van Gogh's picture coincides with the beginnings of the Art Nouveau movement, and it is contemporary with works by other artists, such as Odilon Redon, Munch and Toulouse-Lautrec, who likewise exploited the serpentine line.

But Van Gogh never painted merely for decorative effect. As his letters show, he interpreted the natural world in a highly personal way, projecting his own thoughts and emotions on the things he saw around him. In September 1889, when he was working on several paintings of a man harvesting corn, he wrote of the reaper, 'I see in him the image of death, in the sense that humanity might be what he is reaping. But there's nothing sad in this death, it goes its way in broad daylight with a sun flooding everything with a light of pure gold.' In *A Cornfield with Cypresses* the same sort of symbolism may well apply. The cypresses loom over the cornfield, 'a splash of black in a sunny landscape'. The subject obsessed Van Gogh: he painted several versions of this very painting. The following year when he moved to Auvers-sur-Oise in the north, he again painted the fields of wheat driven by the wind. And when in July 1890 he finally decided to end his life, he went out into the cornfields and shot himself.

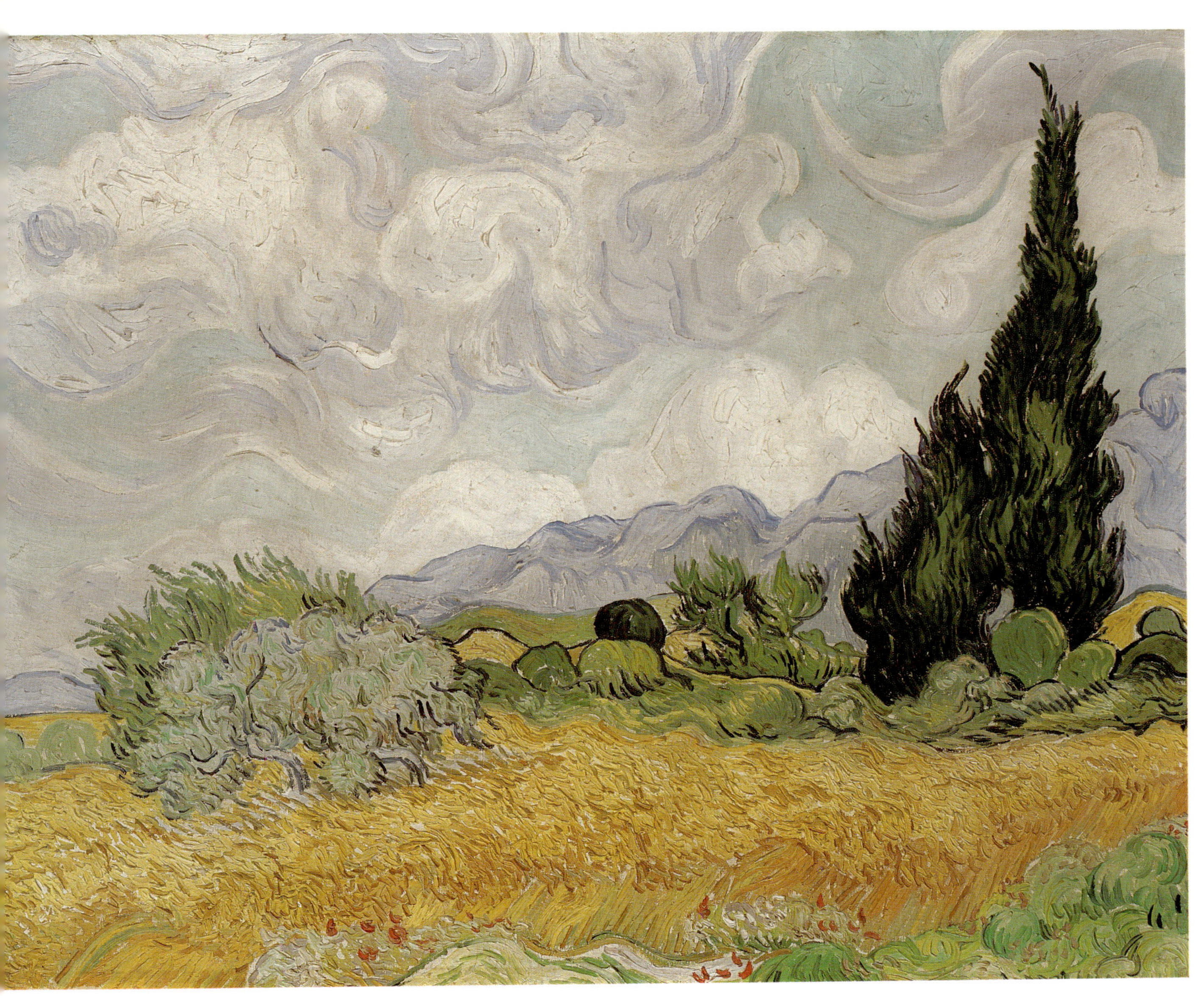

PLATE 38

Paul Gauguin, 1848–1903

Flower Piece (No. 3289)

Signed: P. Gauguin 96
Canvas, 64 × 74 cm.
Purchased 1918

This flower-painting which Gauguin painted in Tahiti in 1896 was sold by his friend Daniel de Monfried to Edgar Degas in 1898. Degas had been quick to recognize the talent of the younger painter, who himself had a strong admiration for Degas' art. While both were gifted colourists, they shared a love of elegant and expressive drawing which shows throughout their work. When Gauguin returned to Paris in 1893 after his first visit to Tahiti, Degas arranged for him an exhibition of the paintings he had done there at the Galerie Durand-Ruel. This met with no success, however, and in 1895 Gauguin returned to Tahiti, never to see France again.

Still-lifes, such as this *Flower Piece*, are uncommon among Gauguin's work. Most of his paintings are of figures and landscapes, often of the two combined, but clearly he was attracted by the decorative potential of the exotic blooms of the Pacific islands. Often they adorn his Tahitian women. Here they are the sole subject and Gauguin intensifies their colour, juxtaposing different shapes of vivid hues to create a powerful decorative group.

Flower-painting had seen a revival in France during the latter part of the nineteenth century, particularly in the work of Manet's friend, Henri Fantin-Latour, but the artist Gauguin approaches most closely in this picture is Odilon Redon. But he could never have known Redon's brilliantly coloured flower-pieces, most of which date from after 1900. Redon, on the other hand, was greatly influenced by Gauguin in his transition to colour in the 1890s, and in 1904, after Gauguin's death, he painted a picture entitled *Homage to Gauguin*, of the artist's head encircled by flowers. It is tempting to wonder whether Redon ever saw this vase of flowers by Gauguin in Degas' collection and whether it helped to inspire the late series of flower-pieces that are the pinnacle of Redon's oeuvre.

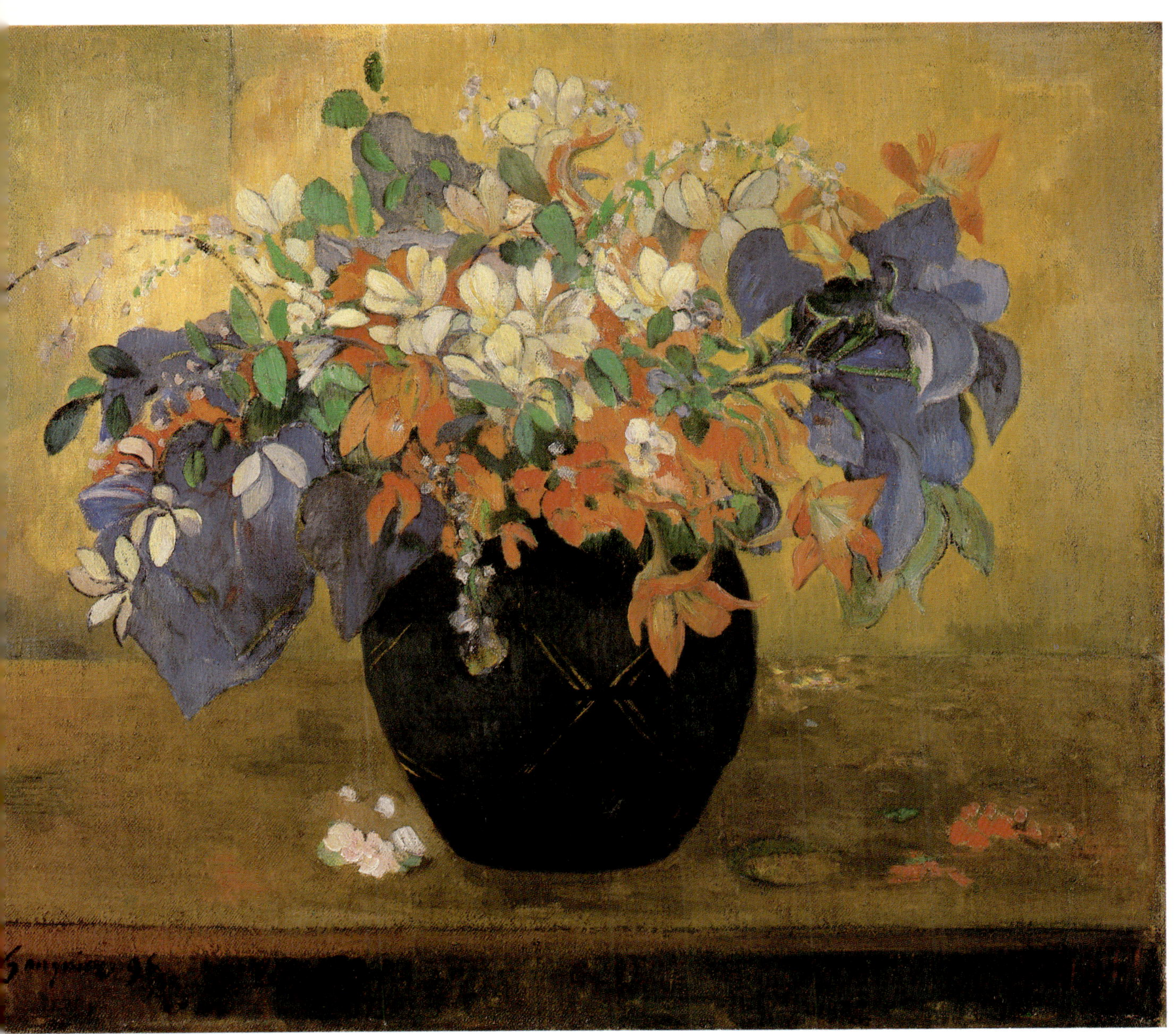

PLATE 39

Gustave Moreau, 1826–1898

St George and the Dragon (No. 6436)

Signed: Gustave Moreau
Canvas, 141 × 96 cm.
Purchased 1976

The story of St George and the Dragon has always been popular among artists, and Moreau's treatment of the subject in this oil painting reveals a large debt to earlier examples. As a leading figure in the French Symbolist movement, who sought to perpetuate the tradition of religious and mythological painting in an age when naturalism had become the dominant force in art, Moreau drew inspiration from Delacroix and from Théodore Chasseriau, the painter of exotic North African subjects and his close friend. From 1857 to 1859 he lived in Italy where he copied examples of Byzantine and Primitive Italian art as well as the Renaissance masters.

This oil painting of St George was painted for Louis Mante in 1890 but the design refers back to a watercolour of the same subject which Moreau painted about twenty years earlier in about 1869. For the group of St George on his rearing horse he drew on Raphael's painting in the Louvre. But the ornamental trappings of the horse and such decorative details as St George's gold halo and the princess's crown look back to earlier Italian art, to Crivelli's gem-encrusted saints, and to Carpaccio's series of murals depicting the legend of St George in the Scuola di San Giorgio degli Schiavoni in Venice, which Moreau studied and copied during his Italian visit.

Moreau's allusions to early Renaissance painting lend a heraldic quality to his image of the warrior saint, emphasizing the spiritual and the mythical in him as against the physical. This incorporeal mood is further developed in the curious figure of the praying princess perched on a rock in front of a pinnacled castle, features which show that like other symbolists of the period Moreau looked at Indian and Persian miniatures and borrowed exotic details from them.

Moreau was an unusual figure and his paintings often met with hostile criticism, which led him to exhibit only intermittently at the Paris Salon, from 1852 until 1880. He nevertheless achieved the honour of being elected to the Academy and in the last six years of his life taught at the Ecole des Beaux-Arts where he won the respect and affection of his pupils, including among them the young Matisse and Rouault.

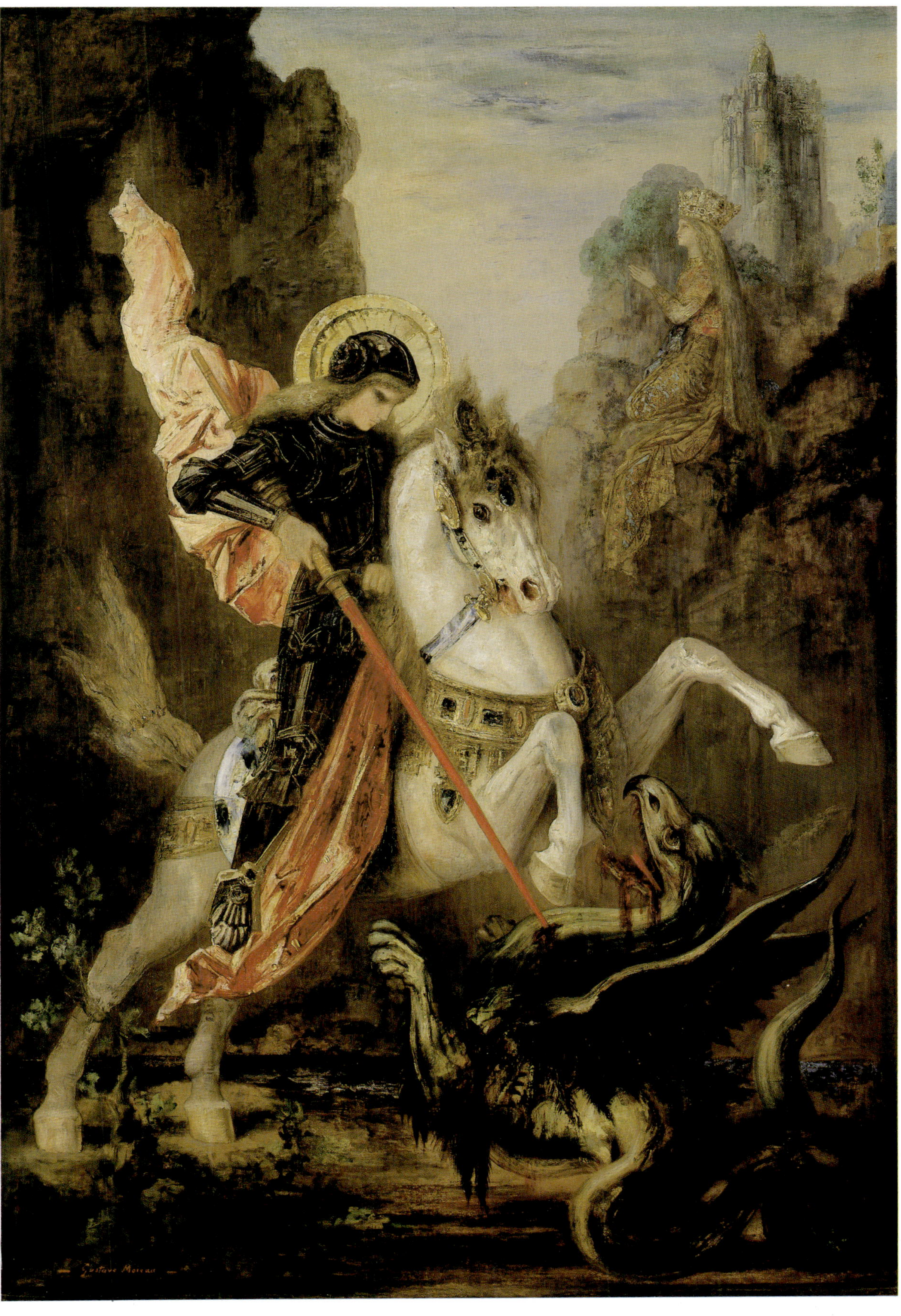
Gustave Moreau

PLATE 40

Henri ('le Douanier') Rousseau, 1844–1910

Tropical Storm with a Tiger (No. 6421)

Signed: Henri Rousseau 1891
Canvas, 130 × 162 cm.
Purchased 1972

Henri Rousseau was about forty when he began to paint seriously, although it was not until 1873 that he retired from his post as a minor inspector at a toll-station on the outskirts of Paris. In 1886 he began to exhibit at the Salon des Indépendants, an annual exhibition organized in rebellion against the official Salon and dominated by such artists as Seurat, Signac and Odilon Redon. Without this jury-free Salon, it is unlikely that Rousseau would ever have been able to exhibit or achieve recognition. He had no formal training as an artist, and his paintings are entirely original in their often absurd subject matter and combinations of flat patterns of colour.

This painting of a tiger stalking through a jungle was exhibited in 1891 under the title *Surpris!*; later Rousseau described it as representing a tiger pursuing explorers. It was the first of the exotic jungle pictures which he continued to produce until his death in 1910, and which he claimed were based on his experiences as a regimental bandsman in Mexico, during the five years he served in the army, from 1863 to 1868. However, it seems that Rousseau never in fact left France and that the fictional Mexican trip was an imaginative embellishment to the already fantastical jungle pictures with their unlikely cast of explorers, cyclists, natives, snake charmers, monkeys and savage beasts.

Rousseau studied the plants and animals at the Jardin des Plantes in Paris and in illustrated books and transferred them to his pictures without much concern for scale. Gigantic leaves and trees, and brilliant colours like those used by Gauguin, lend a wild and exotic air to these invented forests. The highly finished execution, with its precise detail and subtle distinction of colours, Rousseau apparently owed to the academic painters Gérôme and Clément, who he claimed gave him technical advice. And the tiger in *Surpris!* he owed to another artist; it is taken straight from a print after a painting by Delacroix.

Unorthodox though such methods may be, the results are effective and compelling. Except for a small band of admiring poets and painters, including Apollinaire, Léger and Picasso, most people regarded Rousseau as a simpleton, a naive 'primitive'. But in 1910 he wrote to the critic André Dupont, 'I cannot now change my manner, which I have acquired as a result of obstinate toil.' Despite his child-like love of fantasy, Rousseau worked hard to achieve the sophisticated patchwork of shape and colour that is the hallmark of his work.

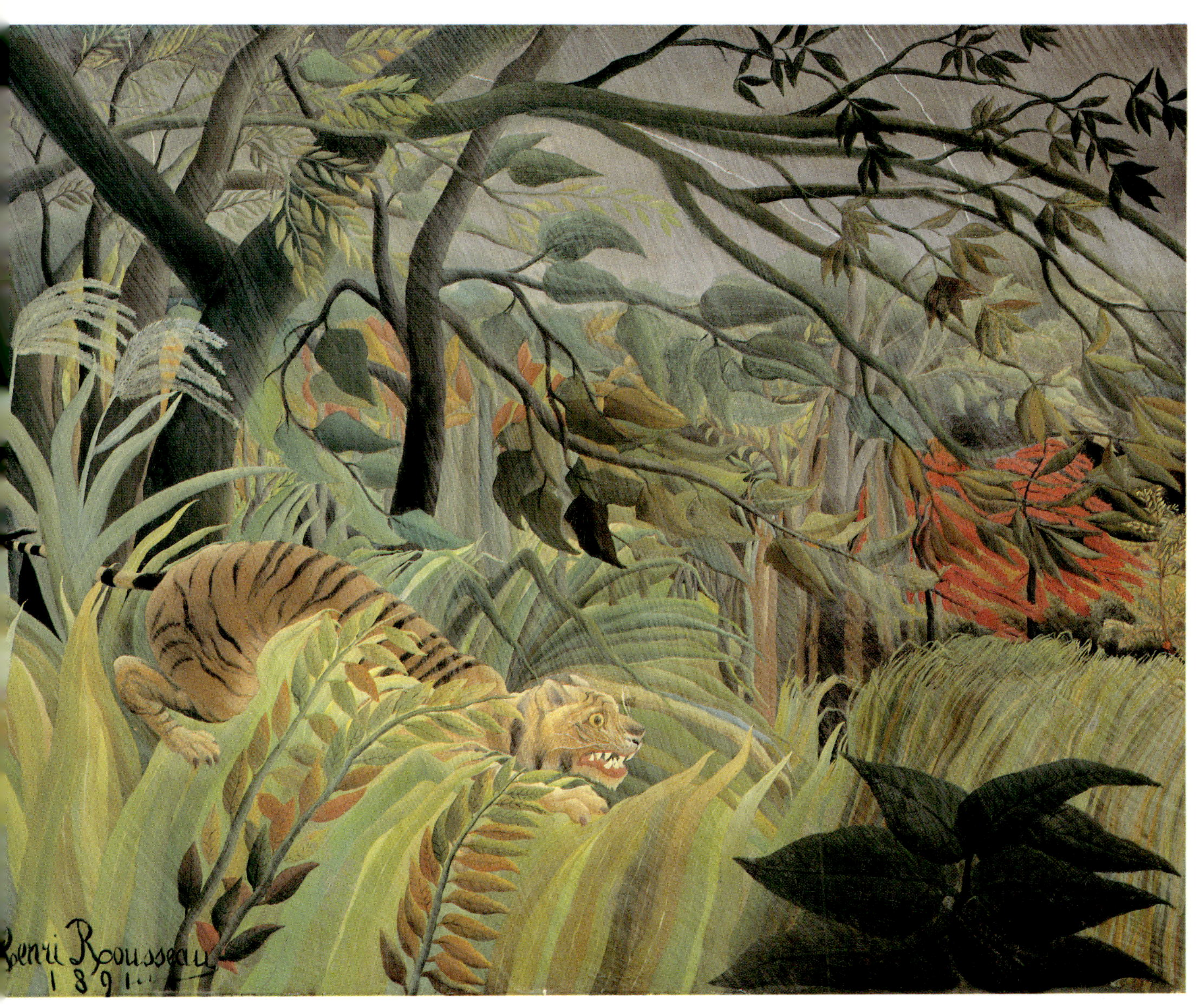

PLATE 41

Claude-Oscar Monet, 1840–1926

The Water Lily Pond (No. 4240)

Signed: Claude Monet 99
Canvas, 88 × 92 cm.
Purchased, Courtauld Fund, 1927

In 1890, when the improved sale of his works had at last put an end to his money troubles, Monet purchased the house at Giverny, a village in the Seine valley between Paris and Rouen, which was to be his home until his death in 1926. The garden he created there was also to provide him with the chief motifs for his painting during the last decades. In it Monet was able to play with colour much as he did on his palette, mixing flowers of different species in masses of varying sizes to create marvellous harmonies that constantly changed with the time and the season. Thus the activities of gardening and painting merged one with another, the flowers in turn providing him with a wealth of visually splendid subjects.

Across the single-track railway at the bottom of Monet's garden was a meadow with a small pond through which ran a tributary of the Epte. In 1893 Monet acquired this piece of land and planted out a water garden across which he built a wooden bridge in the Japanese style, copied from a print that hung in the family dining room. In 1900, at Durand-Ruel's gallery in Paris, he exhibited a series of ten paintings of his water lily pond, with the Japanese bridge, as yet without the canopy of wisteria it later acquired, in the foreground. The composition is in each case the same, with the bridge symmetrically placed arching across the expanse of water which extends into the distance, but the light and colour vary, so that, like the series of paintings of poplars, haystacks, and Rouen cathedral that precede them, the pictures form a decorative whole, united in theme, but each capturing a different mood and revealing a unique aspect of the physiognomy of the place.

In this view the slanting afternoon light throws long shadows across most of the picture, creating cool harmonies of green and mauve. Only in the distance does the sun light up the willows and clumps of irises. Yet the shadows are filled with light, the white bridge is dappled with reflected colour, and between the clumps of water lilies with their silvery-blue leaves and vivid red and white flowers, the trees cast long reflections of bright yellow.

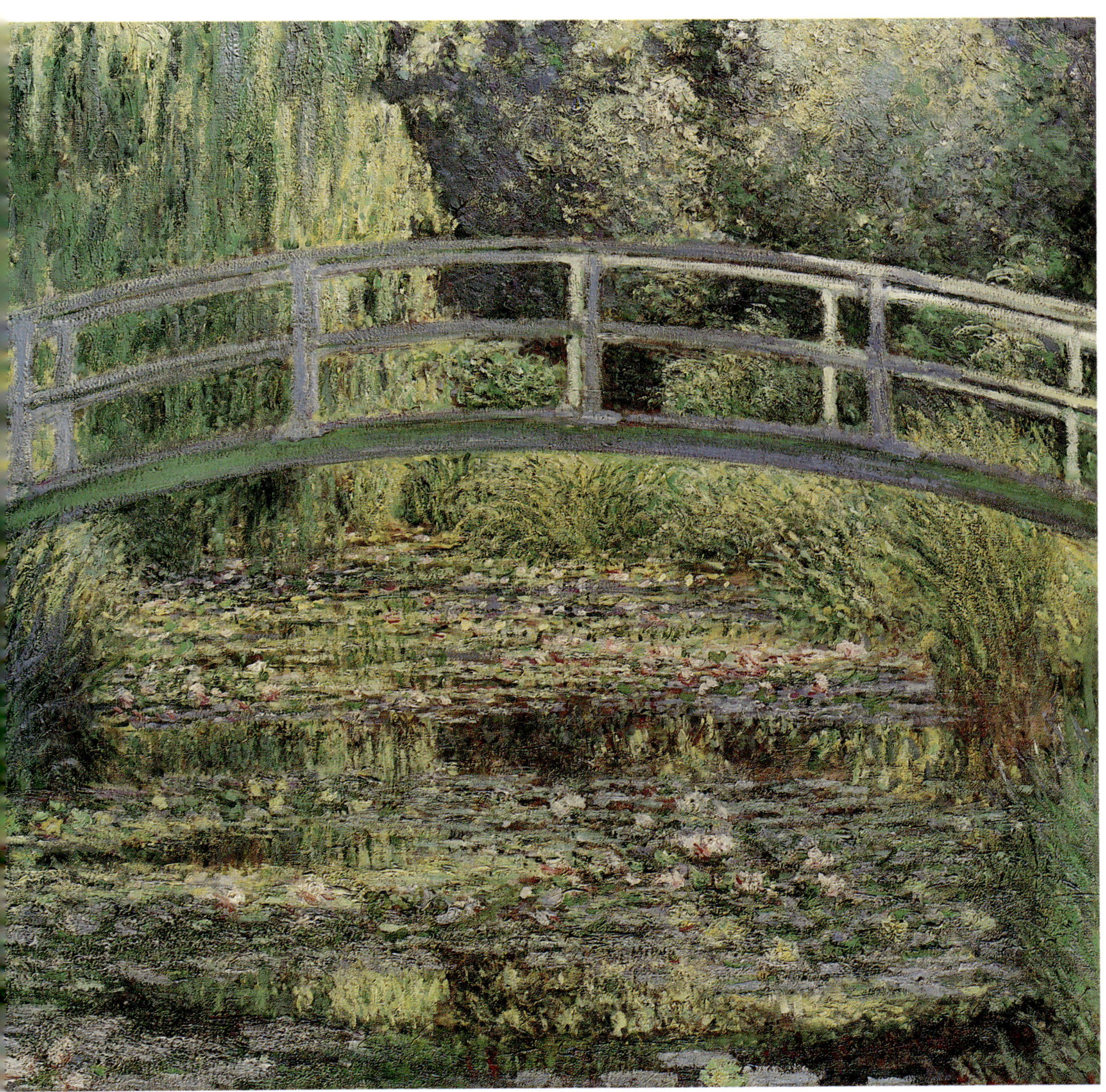

PLATE 42

Camille Pissarro, 1830–1903

Paris. The Boulevard Montmartre at Night (No. 4119)

Canvas, 53 × 65 cm.
Purchased, Courtauld Fund, 1925

Towards the end of the century, having lived and worked in the country for most of his life, Pissarro undertook several series of paintings of urban subjects, in Paris, London, Rouen and at the ports of Dieppe and Le Havre. Apart from any intrinsic interest the sights of the city held for him, Pissarro may also have been drawn to them by considerations of age: they are nearly all painted from windows high up in hotels and apartments which allowed him a variety of good prospects with the minimum discomfort. In Paris, he painted the Place du Carrousel and the Tuileries Gardens from an apartment on the rue de Rivoli; the Pont Neuf and the Louvre from No. 28 Place Dauphine on the Île de la Cité; the Avenue de l'Opéra and the Place du Théâtre Français from the Grand Hôtel du Louvre; and the boulevard Montmartre from the Hôtel de Russie on the corner of the boulevard des Italiens and the rue Drouot. Although he had not before been a painter of city views, Pissarro was in effect taking up an Impressionist theme treated by Monet and Renoir in the 1870s. For Pissarro, with his deeply ingrained feeling for pictorial structure, the prospects of the boulevards and avenues which he gained from the rooms of hotels were admirably suited to his brush, with their strong architectural features and deep perspectival recession.

This evocative sketch of the boulevard Montmartre is one of a series of views of this particular street which Pissarro painted in 1897, but it is unique in being the only night scene he ever made. It is not as fully elaborated as the other views. It is unsigned and Pissarro does not appear to have exhibited it. It nevertheless conveys all the atmosphere of a busy street on a wet winter's evening. Lights gleam from shops and windows and from the lines of carriages, and shimmer on the wet pavements. A turgid, inky sky lowers over the animated thoroughfare and the glowing street lamps create a nimbus of darkness around them.

The scene is brilliantly observed, and skilfully depicted by the briefest painterly shorthand. Rows of windows and crowds of pedestrians are summarily conveyed by single strokes of paint; a vigorous scribble indicates the rows of trees lining the boulevard; and touches of thick creamy impasto stand for points of light, shining out on the gloom. And to this atmospheric description Pissarro adds the suggestion of movement, the lines of apartment buildings, vehicles, trees, lamps and even the sky itself converging dynamically where the street disappears into the night.

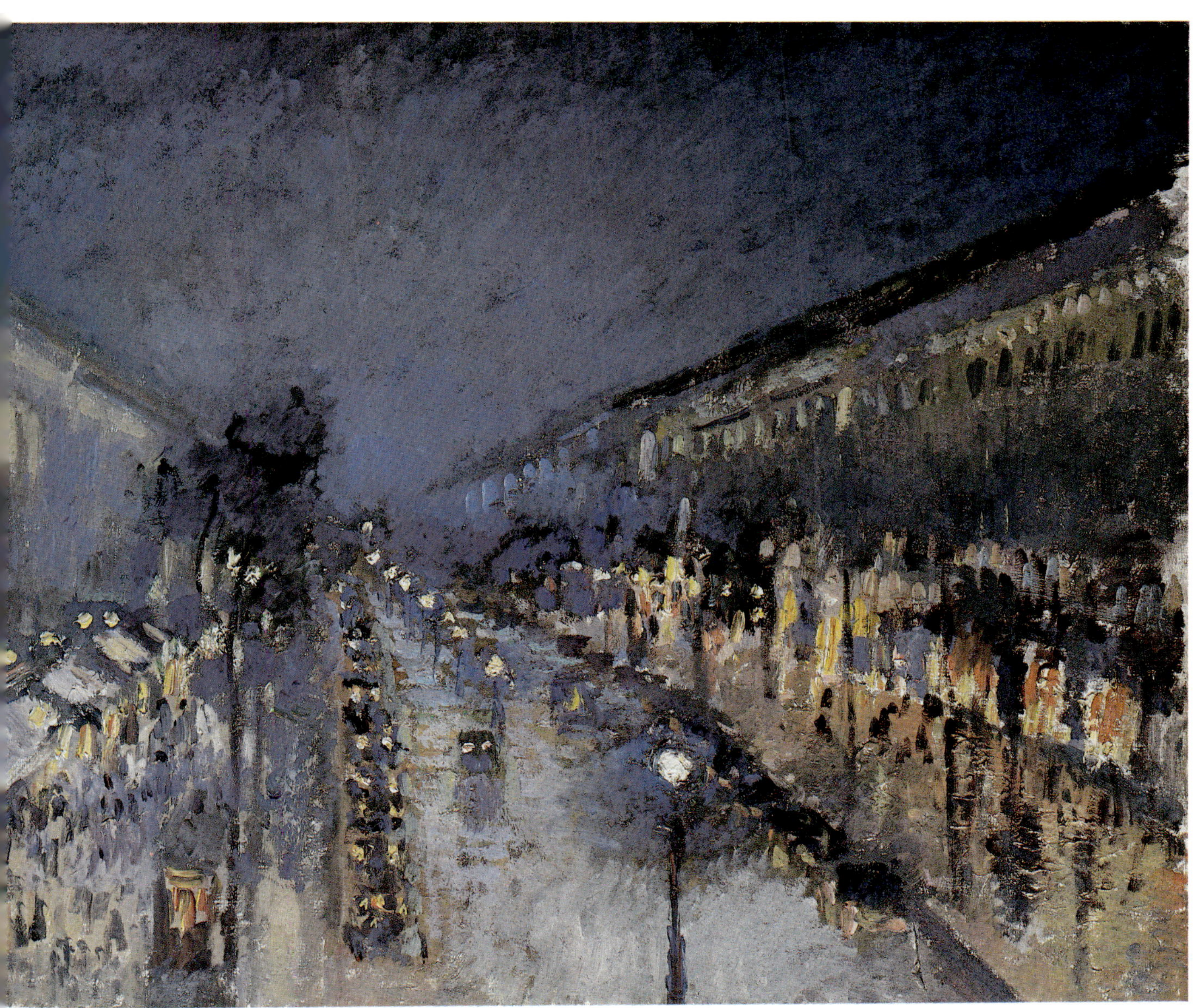

PLATE 43

Paul Cézanne, 1839–1906

An Old Woman with a Rosary (No. 6195)

Canvas, 81 × 65 cm.
Purchased 1953

It is tempting to wonder how the young Cézanne, with his temperamental inclination towards scenes of torment and suffering, would have treated this subject. The sitter, as described by Cézanne to Joachim Gasquet, the first owner of the picture, was an old nun who, having lost her faith and escaped from her convent at the age of seventy, wandered aimlessly until the painter took her on as a servant. She would mumble her prayers, and tell lies, but out of charity he would turn a blind eye to her little deceptions. In Cézanne's portrayal of her there is none of the melodrama of his early works. She is shown slightly bowed, her hands automatically fingering a rosary as perhaps she murmurs her prayers. Cézanne expresses his sympathy for the feeble-minded old woman by depicting all this, not with the uncontrolled emotion of his early years, but with detachment and respect for her individuality as a person.

Nevertheless the painting is boldly executed in a vigorous technique of blocks of colour, subtly modulated to represent the articulation of volumes. The old woman has a monumental solidity, the deeply modelled face and sculpted cap dominating the broad pyramid of her shoulders and the chunky hands, like lumps of carved rock. And to accentuate the form of the arms and torso, Cézanne has employed a darker drawing of blue against the solid colour of the shawl. The whole is unremittingly sombre, with the same intense shades of blue and purple extended throughout the background.

According to Gasquet the picture was painted at the Jas de Bouffan, Cézanne's family house near Aix, in 1896. In the book he published on the artist in 1921 he describes how he found the picture lying on the floor of Cézanne's studio with a pipe dripping on it, and the lower left corner of the picture does in fact bear marks caused by splashing water or steam.

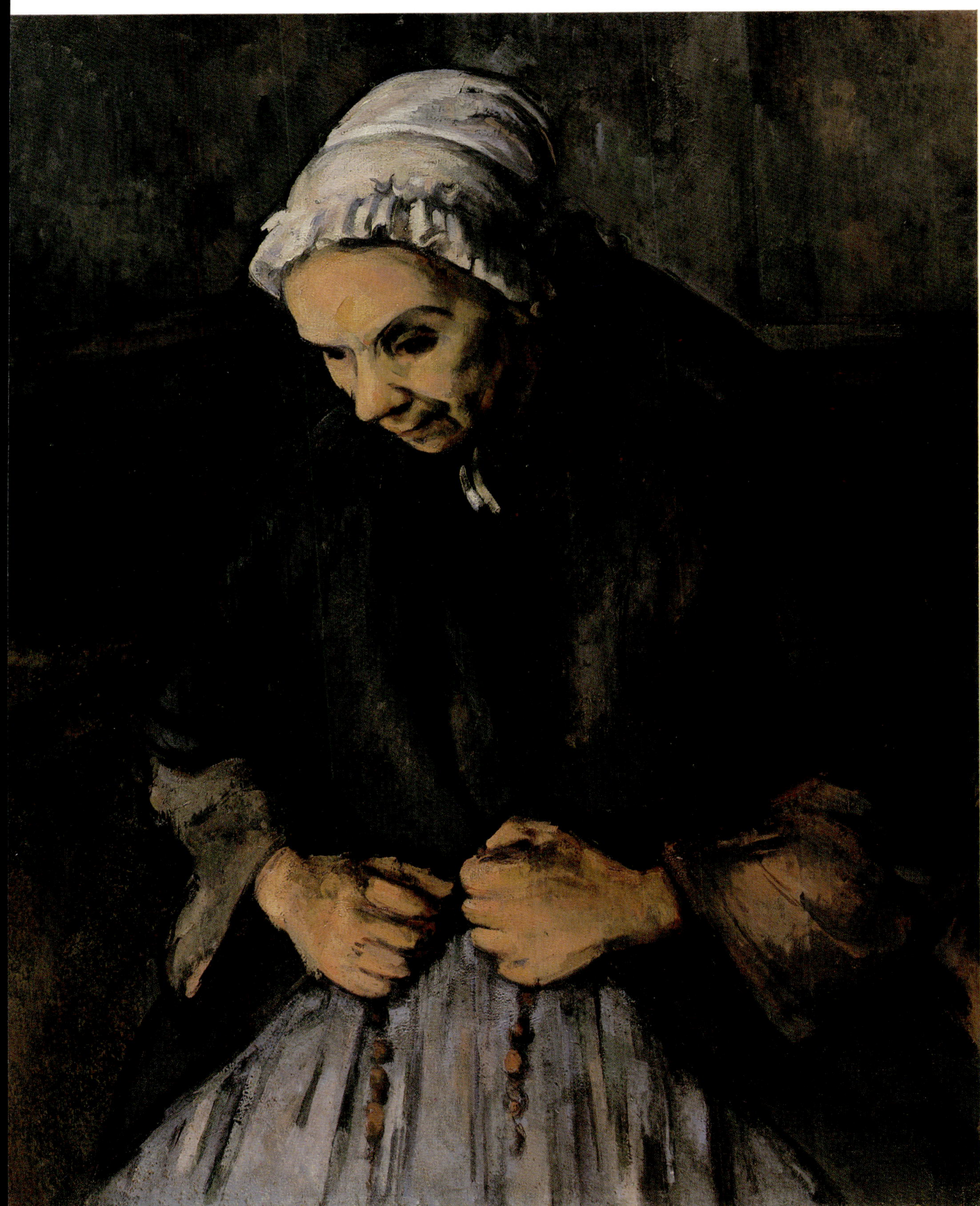

PLATE 44

Paul Cézanne, 1839–1906

Bathers (No. 6359)

Canvas, 136 × 196 cm.
Purchased 1964

Although most of Cézanne's mature work consists of landscapes, still-lifes and figure subjects painted and drawn from the life, he never lost that interest in imaginative compositions with nude figures, evident in some of his earliest romantically-inspired works. At the 1874 Impressionist exhibition he showed a little oil sketch called *A Modern Olympia* which seems to parody Delacroix and Manet and also to poke fun at himself, since it includes a small bald-headed man gazing admiringly at a nude on a bed.

Nevertheless Cézanne's abiding interest in such subjects reveals a serious concern with earlier art. As a painter he wished not only to reinterpret nature in his own way, but also to contribute to the classical tradition by adding his own interpretations of traditional themes. Small pictures with bathers appear in his work from the 1870s, but not until the end of his life, when perhaps he at last felt equal to the task, did he attempt the theme on a grand scale, in three large canvases of women bathers: the one illustrated here in the National Gallery, another of similar size in the Barnes Foundation at Merion, Pennsylvania, and a third, larger painting in the Philadelphia Museum. In none of these is a precise subject indicated, although the theme of Diana and her nymphs comes readily to mind in looking at them. But they all share a monumentality and dignity which directly link them to the mythological painting of the Renaissance, particularly to Titian's great canvases of *Diana and Actaeon* and *Diana and Callisto*.

The genesis of Cézanne's three canvases is not entirely clear from the surviving evidence. A photograph taken by Emile Bernard in 1904 shows Cézanne seated in front of the Barnes version, and it seems he was working on this canvas which shows signs of frequent revision and overpainting from 1895 until 1906. The National Gallery version seems to have been the next to be undertaken, begun in about 1898 or 99 and finished in 1905. The Philadelphia version which relates most closely in composition to the London version must have been painted quite quickly in the last months of the artist's life in 1906. It was left unfinished, with parts of the canvas still showing through.

The National Gallery picture is in many respects the simplest and the strongest. A frieze of large-limbed bathers, their faces mask-like or turned away, occupy the whole of the middle part of the painting, inclining together like a massive pyramid. As heavy as rock, they become a part of nature itself, the tones of their flesh echoing the earth-colours of the foreground and the blues of the sky. Well might such a picture appeal to a sculptor: Henry Moore has described the first sight of this painting as one of 'the most intense moments of visual emotion of my life'.

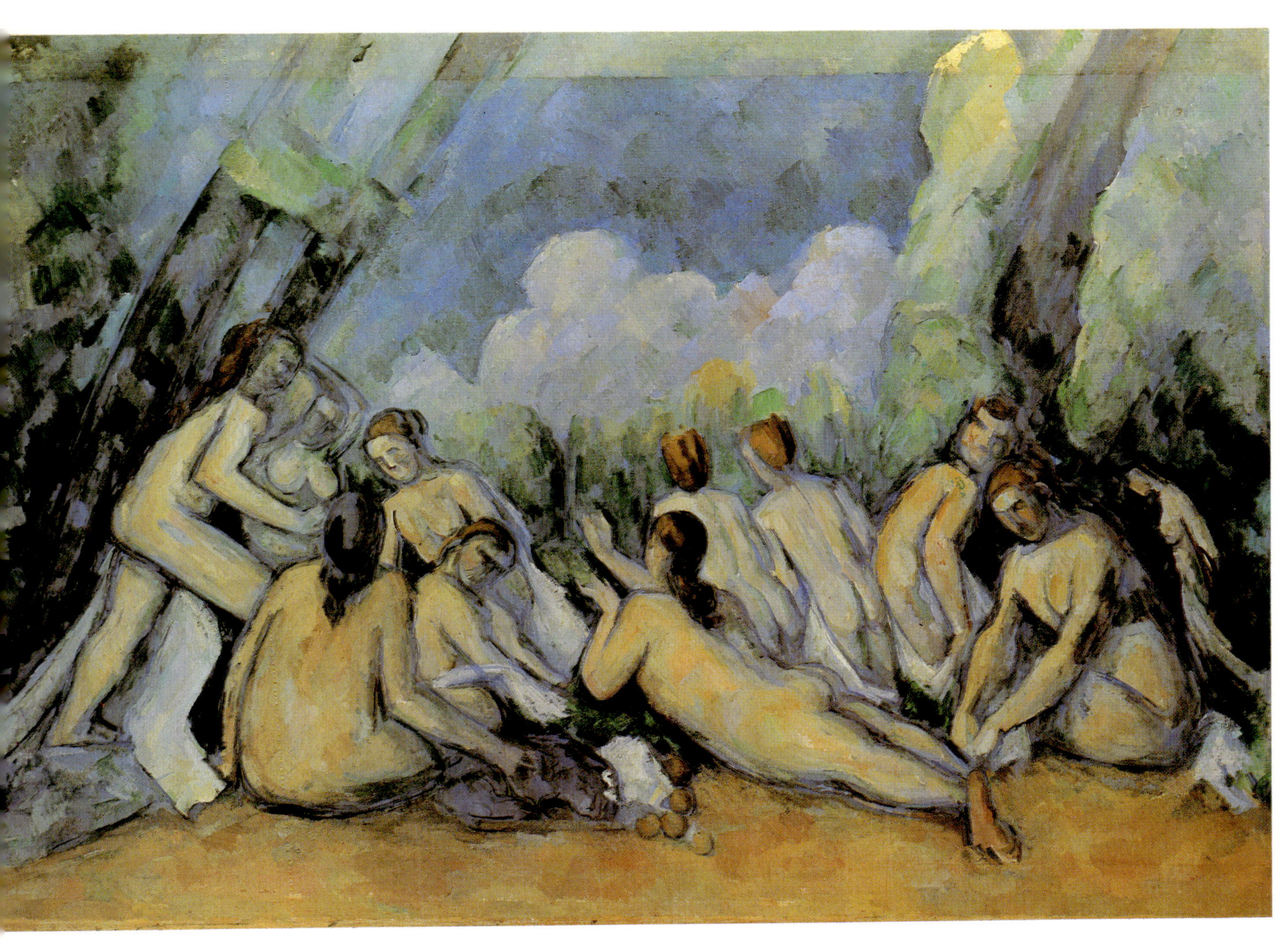

PLATE 45

Edouard Vuillard, 1868–1940

The Chimneypiece (No. 3271)

Signed: E. Vuillard 1905
Pasteboard, 51 × 77 cm.
Lane Bequest, 1917

Vuillard was never so much at ease as with the most familiar of subject matter. During the 1890s he formed part of an *avant-garde* set of painters called Les Nabis or The Prophets, including Paul Serusier, Maurice Denis, Paul Ranson, and Pierre Bonnard, who set out to give expression to 'the Idea' by the 'deformation' of nature, in other words to use pattern and distortion to suggest the psychological meanings underlying appearances. To do so they adopted a flat decorative mode of painting, based on the various influences of Gauguin and the Pont-Aven group, Japanese prints, primitive sculpture and Symbolist painting. By the end of the decade, however, Vuillard had tired of the overtly spiritual and philosophical character of Nabis art, and with Bonnard returned to a more naturalistic style. As Nabis they had already established a preference for '*Intimiste*' themes – the familiar scenes of domestic life. They now chose to represent them with far greater fidelity to nature, but with no less a suggestive intimacy.

The Chimneypiece, which dates from 1905, is like a corner of a Degas, the clutter of objects littering the mantelpiece and decorating the corner of the room painted with great truth to appearances, but also with the freedom and brevity of an Impressionist. Yet even by Impressionist standards it is fragmentary, a close-up of a fireplace seen at such close quarters that the end of the marble mantelpiece almost blocks our vision, and the front disappears in steep recession. By honing in on such detail, Vuillard excludes most of the room, leaving it to suggestion and the imagination. He recaptures the innocence of childhood vision which sees each little thing with crystal clarity as though it were a world in itself, and seldom grasps the whole. The ordinary objects of everyday life – a glass of wild flowers, medicine bottles, laundry airing by the fire – take on a magical sense of novelty within the richly patterned interior.

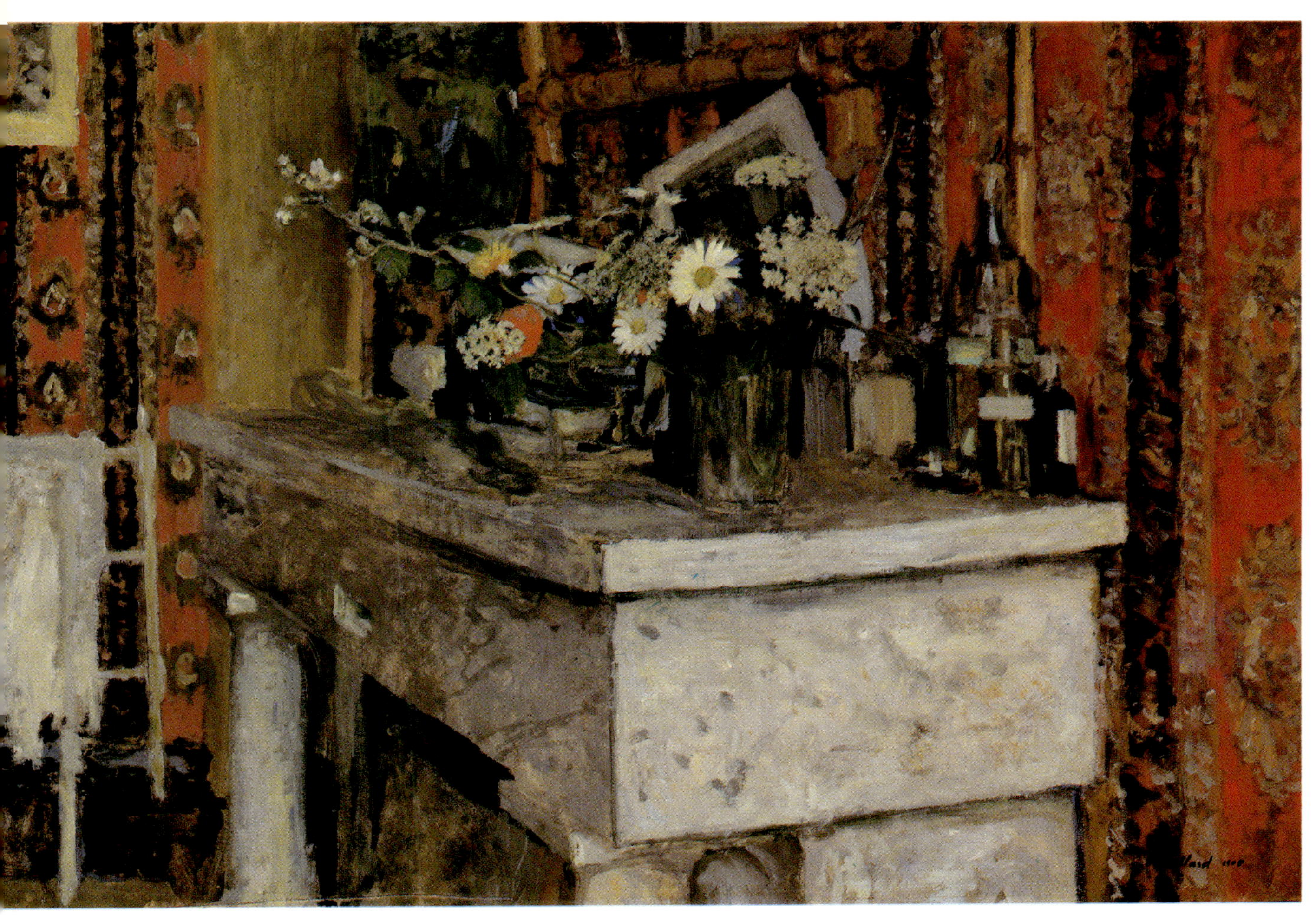

PLATE 46

Odilon Redon, 1840–1916

Ophelia among the Flowers (No. 6438)

Pastel, 64 × 91 cm.
Purchased, 1977

Odilon Redon is a curious figure in the history of nineteenth-century painting. Born in 1840, the same year as Monet, he remained obscure and aloof from the whole naturalistic current of Realism and Impressionism, concentrating on black and white work – charcoal drawings, etchings and lithographs of macabre imaginary subjects. Not until after 1880 was his work noticed, firstly by the *avant-garde* literary set of Symbolists, and gradually by other, younger artists, including Gauguin, Emile Bernard and the group known as the Nabis. It was under their influence that Redon gradually turned from the black and white work, his '*noirs*' as he called them, to colour. And with the change to brightly coloured oils and pastels came a dramatic transformation of mood, to joyful and optimistic themes after years of sinister nightmares.

Ophelia among the Flowers, the only work by Redon in the Collection, may seem, on the face of it, a tragic subject. Derived from Shakespeare, the picture represents the drowned Ophelia, in profile, against a landscape with a fantastic wreath of flowers burgeoning above her. But the effect is far from dismal or oppressive. Ophelia's face is expressive of a spiritual calm, and the flowers, brilliantly hued blooms of no known species, seem projections of her trance-like state, the visions of a dreamer.

The creation of the picture itself, with its elaborate pastel hatchings and merging colours, was not entirely premeditated. It seems that the drawing was started as a simple flower-piece, a favourite subject of the artist, showing blooms in a blue vase on a brown table. And then in response to the stimulus of the drawing and of his imagination, Redon turned the paper on its side and added the face of Ophelia, and the suggestion of a landscape background. He grasped the possibility of Shakespeare's mad heroine, who drowned laden with 'fantastic garlands', being shown to represent the type of the visionary artist who, with closed eyes, perceives an order of beauty which transcends everyday reality.

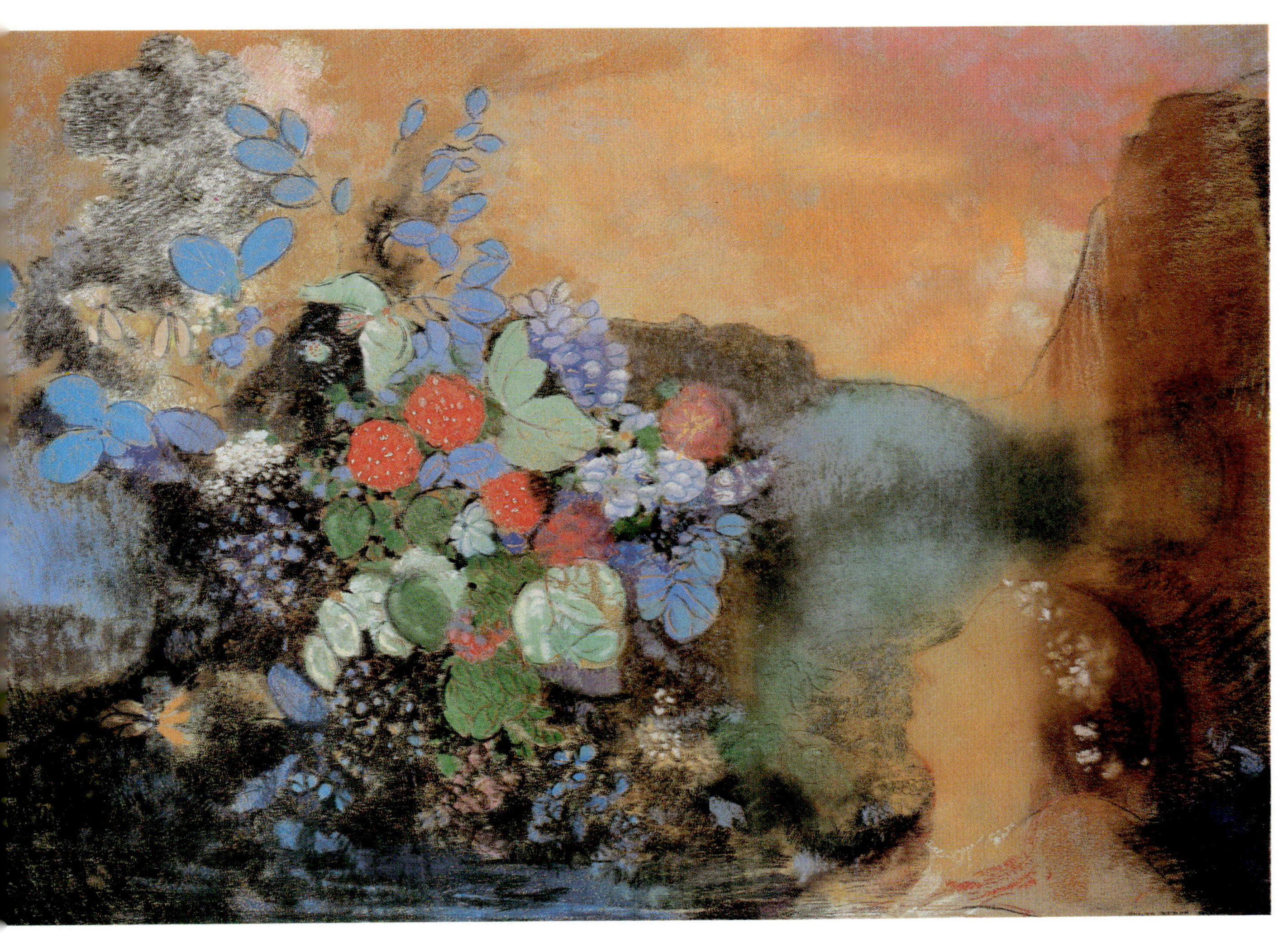

PLATE 47

Henri Matisse, 1869–1954

Portrait of Greta Moll (No. 6450)

Signed: Henri Matisse 1908
Canvas, 93 × 73 cm.
Purchased 1979

Besides being painters themselves, Greta Moll, who was born in Mulhouse in 1884, and her German husband, Oskar Moll, were for a time pupils of Matisse and avid collectors of his work. It was around Christmas of 1907 that Matisse asked to paint Frau Moll, having seen in reproduction and disliked a portrait of her by Louis Corinth. Greta Moll later described how she sat for ten sessions, three hours each early in 1908, and how Matisse conceived the daring idea of showing her against a boldly figured blue and white fabric: *'ça prend une grandeur merveilleuse,'* he assured her. Each time he altered one colour, he felt forced to change the entire colour scheme; the greenish blouse was at one time lavender white, and the black skirt, yellowish green. But even when the sittings were complete Matisse was dissatisfied. His final inspiration came from a portrait of a woman by Veronese, in the Louvre. He borrowed the plump arms for his portrait, and once again revised the picture. 'Later on I did not notice it any more,' Greta recalled, 'but at first the fat arms and the heavy eyebrows I had got bothered me.'

The finished portrait betrays no sign of labour. It is vigorously painted with broad and confident strokes of the brush. The flowered cotton print was indeed a favourite studio prop of Matisse in the early years of the century; it reappears in numerous paintings of the period, including the famous *Harmony in Red* (originally *Harmony in Blue*) now in the Hermitage, Leningrad. But he rarely employed it so daringly or so dangerously, as here. Greta's head is enveloped by the sweeping strokes of blue, and yet survives by virtue of the firm modelling of the features, and the warm colouring of her red hair and pink complexion, which complements the blues of the backdrop. It is a virtuoso achievement of artistry, and also a wonderful compliment to the sitter. The energetic movement of the design seems to emanate from her face, and to be an extension of her patently warm and youthful character, which Matisse had complained the portrait by the German Corinth had failed to capture.

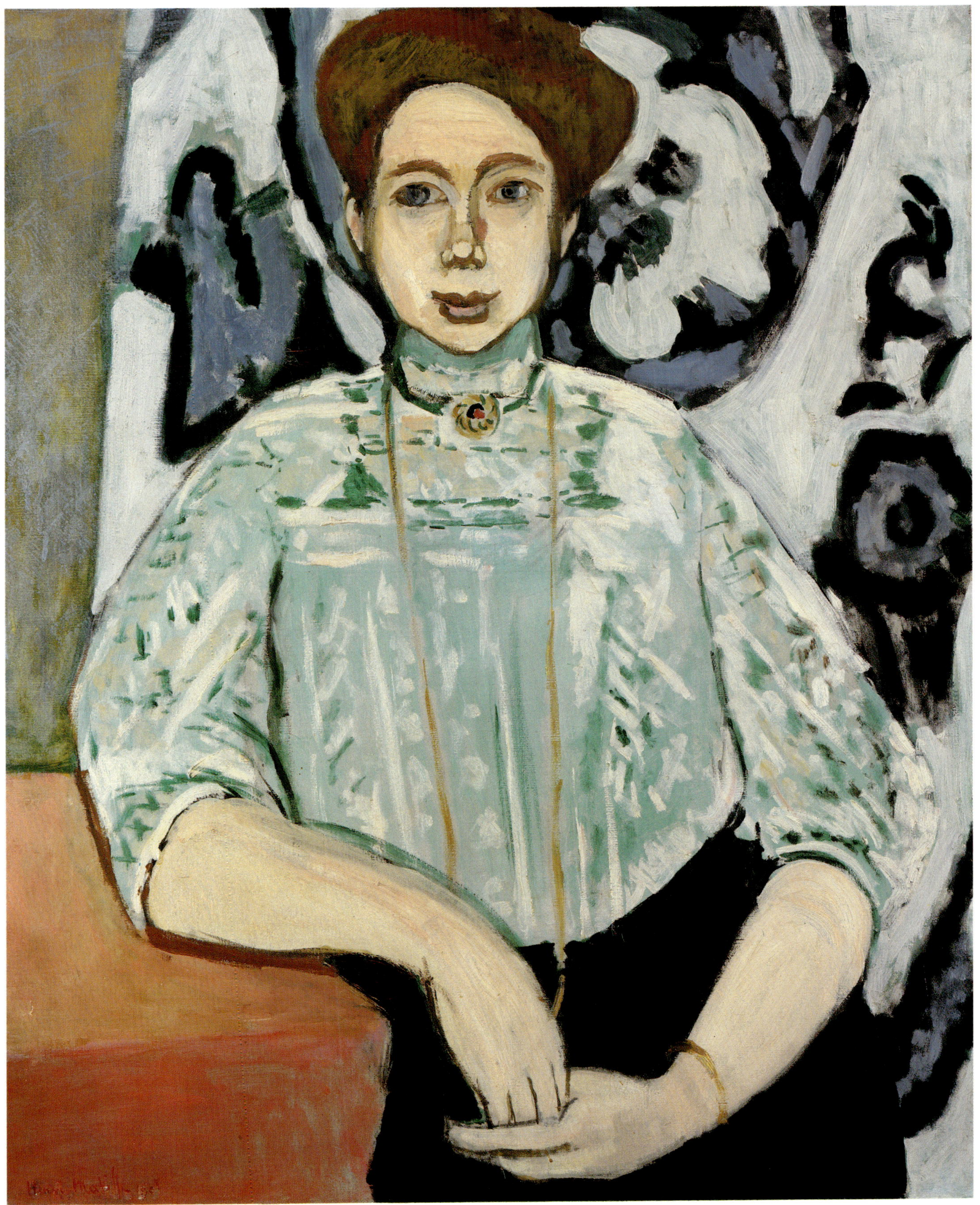

PLATE 48

Pablo Picasso, 1881–1973

Bowl of Fruit, Bottle and Violin (No. 6449)

Signed: Picasso
Canvas, 92 × 73 cm.
Purchased 1979

Although not the latest work in the Collection, this Cubist still-life of 1914 is in many respects the most modern. Combining areas of strong flat colour, spotted textures, bare canvas and sand to produce a novel decorative effect, it emphasizes the picture surface and the physical media used by the artist at the expense of pictorial illusion in a way that breaks decisively with most of what is represented in this book.

At the time when he painted this picture Picasso, like his friend Braque, was seeking ways of revitalizing the language of Cubism. Their experiments over the preceding few years with analytical Cubism had led to densely worked, sombrely coloured pictures, in which few clues remain amid the monochrome fragments of form to indicate the subject. The neutral tones of analytical Cubism are retained in parts of this painting, in the background and in the superimposed facets of the violin in the centre, but the forms are stronger and more explicit, and the subject can be identified without too much difficulty. Various objects, including those of the title, are crowded on to a circular topped table, the bulbous legs of which protrude beneath a fringed tablecloth. The densely packed composition culminates at the top of the canvas, in the brilliantly coloured, stemmed dish of fruit.

Visually more decorative and appealing than the earlier Cubist works, the picture shows a greater freedom of conception and execution. Some parts have clearly been changed or hastily painted out in the course of execution, and the paint is boldly applied in large unmodulated patches or broad freely sketched strokes. Nevertheless, while many of the so-called synthetic cubist pictures which Picasso painted in 1914–15 are playful in their use of visual puns, collage and other unexpected devices, this painting is unusually dignified. It is classical in its strongly centralized arrangement, and in its grasp of generalized form shows to an uncommon degree Picasso's debt to Cézanne.

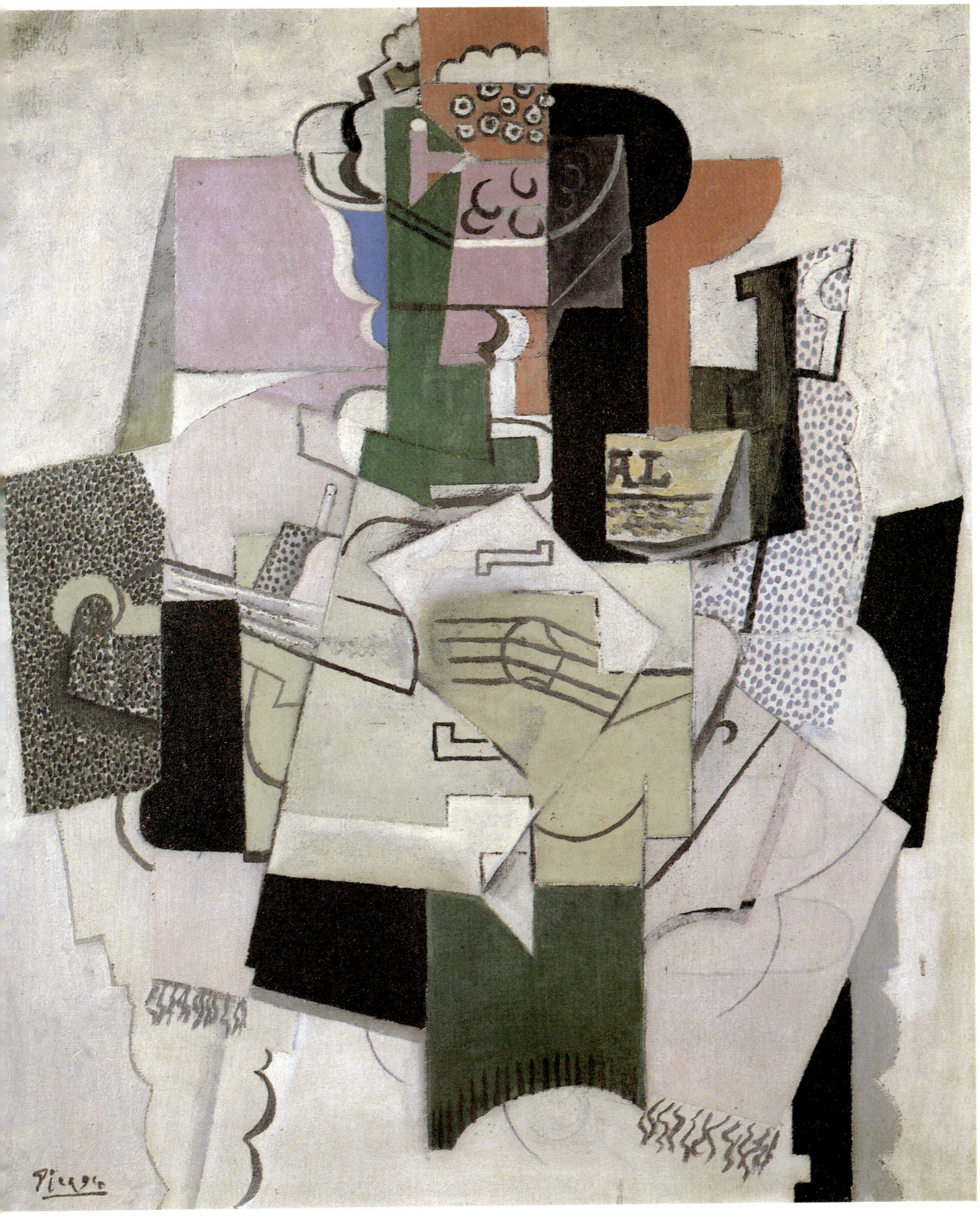
AL

PLATES 49 and 50

Pierre-Auguste Renoir, 1841–1919

Dancing Girl with Tambourine and *Dancing Girl with Castanets*

Both signed: Renoir. 09. (Nos. 6317 and 6318)

Canvas, each 155 × 65 cm.

Purchased 1961

Towards the end of his life Renoir abandoned the tight, linear style which he had adopted following his visit to Italy in 1881 and returned to the rounded forms, sensuous paintwork and merging colours of his earlier work. 'He never proceeded with angles or lines,' wrote the painter's son Jean of his father's technique in old age. 'His "handwriting" was rounded as if following the contour of a young woman's belly.' And the favourite theme of Renoir's old age was the nude, large-limbed, plump women, like ripe fruit, that look back not to Ingres and Raphael, but to Delacroix and Boucher.

The achievement of Renoir's late years, when the kind climate of the south had induced him to settle at Cagnes, on the Mediterranean coast, is all the more remarkable in view of his declining health. After 1900 he became increasingly crippled by arthritis, until the paintbrushes had to be strapped to his hand. In order for him to reach the upper sections of these two large canvases of dancers, his chair had to be erected on trestles. Nevertheless the transparent paintwork with its flickering highlights betrays no sign of the artist's disability.

The pair of dancers was commissioned by Maurice Gangnat, a collector whom Renoir considered had a better eye for his paintings than any man alive. 'His feeling for painting was astounding,' Jean Renoir recalled. 'Whenever he entered the studio his gaze always fell immediately on the canvas Renoir considered his best.' The paintings were designed for the dining room of Gangnat's Paris apartment at 24, avenue de Friedland, where they were intended to flank a fireplace surmounted by a mirror. At first Renoir planned to paint girls bearing dishes of food, but the idea was abandoned on the grounds that the family might move house, as in due course they did. A model called Georgette Pigeot posed for both canvases, but for the head of the *Dancing Girl with Castanets* Renoir used the dark-haired Gabrielle, a cousin of his wife who lived with them as the children's nurse and who was his favourite model.

The paintings are conceived as decorations, each complementing the other. The girls face one another and each is posed against the same indistinct greenish ground. The predominant colour in one is pink, in the other blue, while both have similar exotic accoutrements of fancily worked boleros, gauzy skirts, pointed slippers and flowers. The direct descendants of Delacroix's North African harem girls, these dancers were themselves to be the inspiration of the odalisques of Henri Matisse.

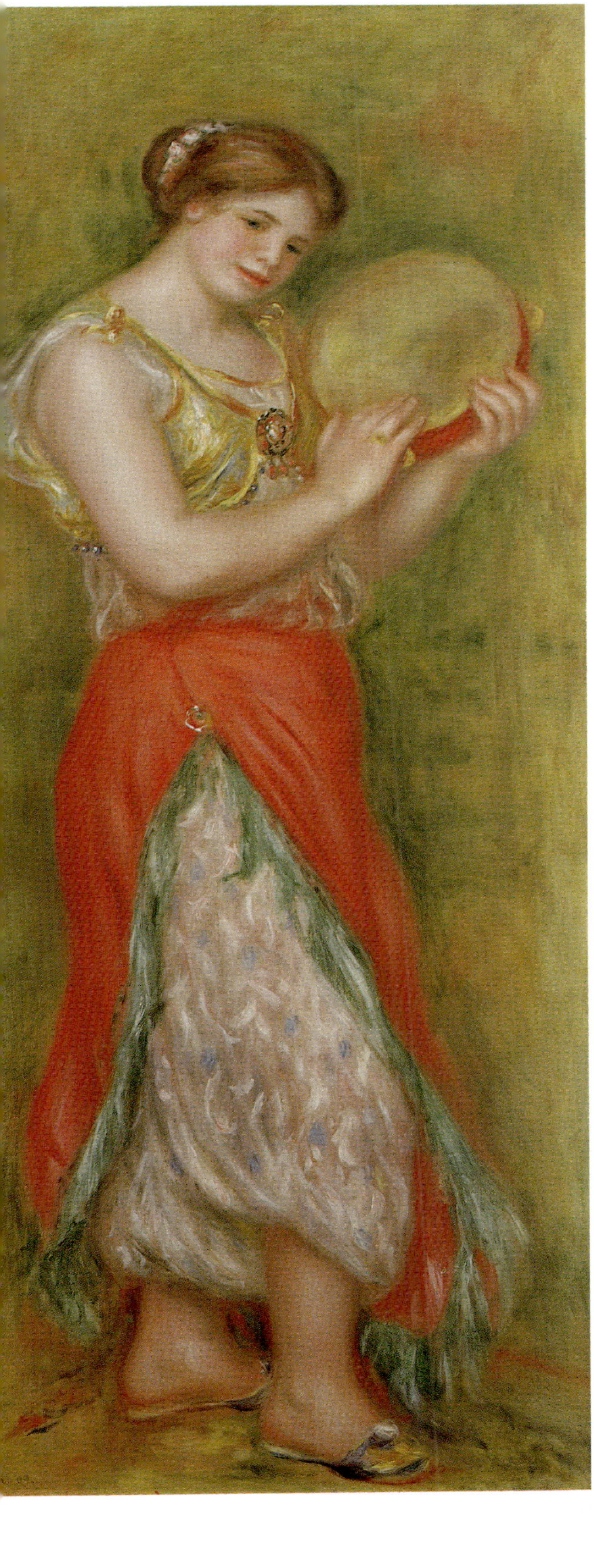

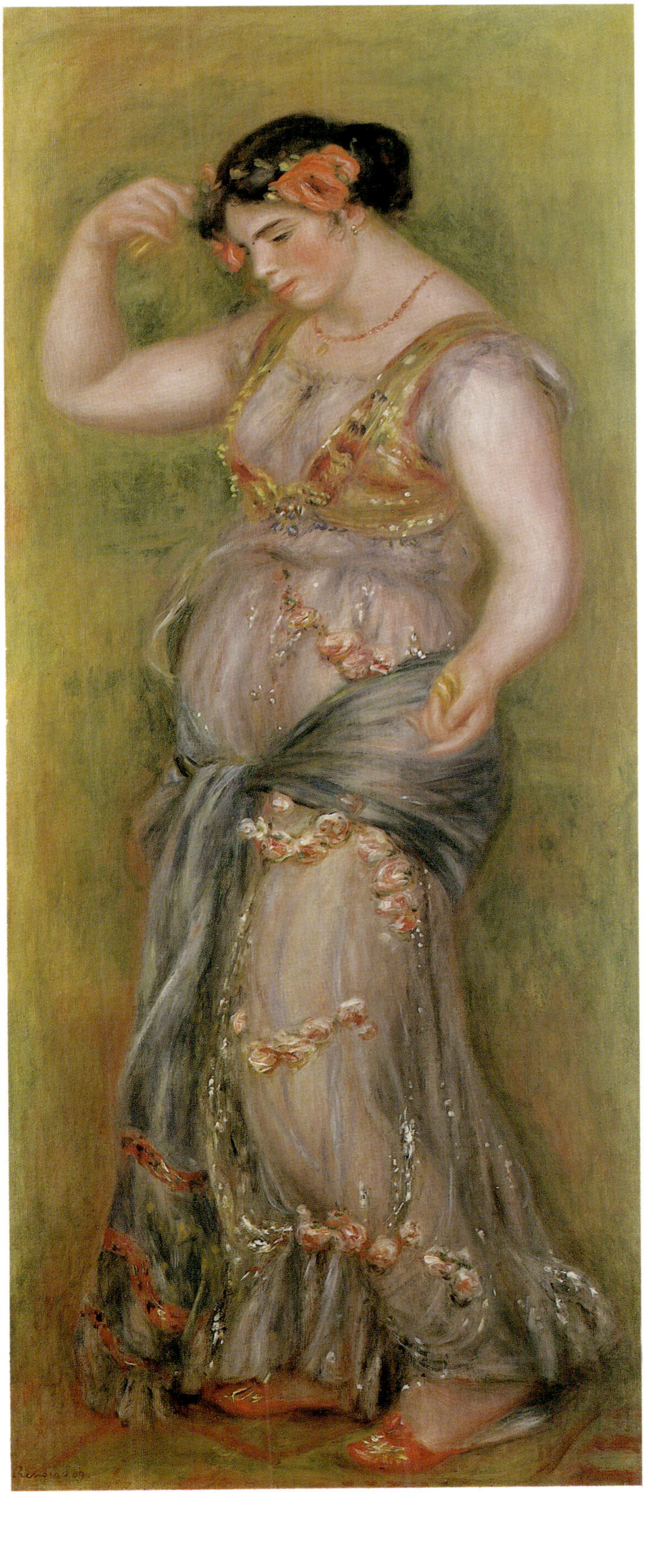

PLATE 51

Claude-Oscar Monet, 1840–1926

Water Lilies (No. 6343)

Stamped: Claude Monet
Canvas, 200 × 427 cm.
Purchased 1963

From the time he purchased the land below his garden at Giverny to make a water lily pond in 1893, Monet was obsessed by the idea of painting the flower-studded surface of the water with its ever-changing reflections. He exhibited a first series of pictures of the pond in 1900 (see Plate 41), a second was shown in 1909, and this enormous canvas belongs to a third group begun in about 1916. As the vision of water lilies developed in Monet's mind, so the physical counterpart had to expand to meet his demands. The pond was enlarged twice, once in 1901 and again in 1910, and as he increased the size of his canvases, so Monet built a second and finally a third enormous studio to accommodate them.

The construction of the final studio and the creation of the large, late paintings was connected with a project which had formed in Monet's mind as early as 1909, to donate to the French nation a series of paintings which would constitute a monumental decorative scheme. 'Enveloping all the walls in its unity, it would produce the illusion of an endless whole, of water without horizon or bank. Nerves tense from work would relax there, following the restful example of still waters, and to him who lived with it, the room would offer the asylum of a peaceable meditation at the centre of a flowering aquarium.' Thus Monet's vision was reported by the critic Roger Marx. Originally the series of paintings was intended for the Musée Rodin at the Hôtel Biron in Paris, but finally two special rooms were constructed for it to Monet's design in the Orangerie, where in 1927, following his death, the huge canvases were installed.

This painting of water lilies is one that Monet produced at the same time as the Orangerie decorations and is on a canvas of the same height. Painted entirely in the studio from studies and from his memory of the pond, it represents the final stage in Monet's move towards a more decorative and contemplative concept of painting. In view of its huge scale, it becomes an imposing object in its own right, a large screen of merging colour, not unlike the decorative Japanese screens that he so admired. It excludes all view of bank and horizon and takes us close to the water's surface, which is suffused by a golden light. The paint is thickly applied in layer upon layer of broad, swirling patterns, creating a dense harmony of different shades of violet and greenish-yellow. Yet it is not entirely without definition. The pools of water lilies recede into the distance across the top of the canvas while, as in opposition to them, the vague reflections of trees on the opposite bank form a veil of colour which seems to float parallel to the picture plane, below the water's surface. Moving among these merging forms, the eye shifts from the steeply inclined surface of the pond to the illusion of foliage deep in space, and back again, endlessly perpetuating this luminous moment of time.

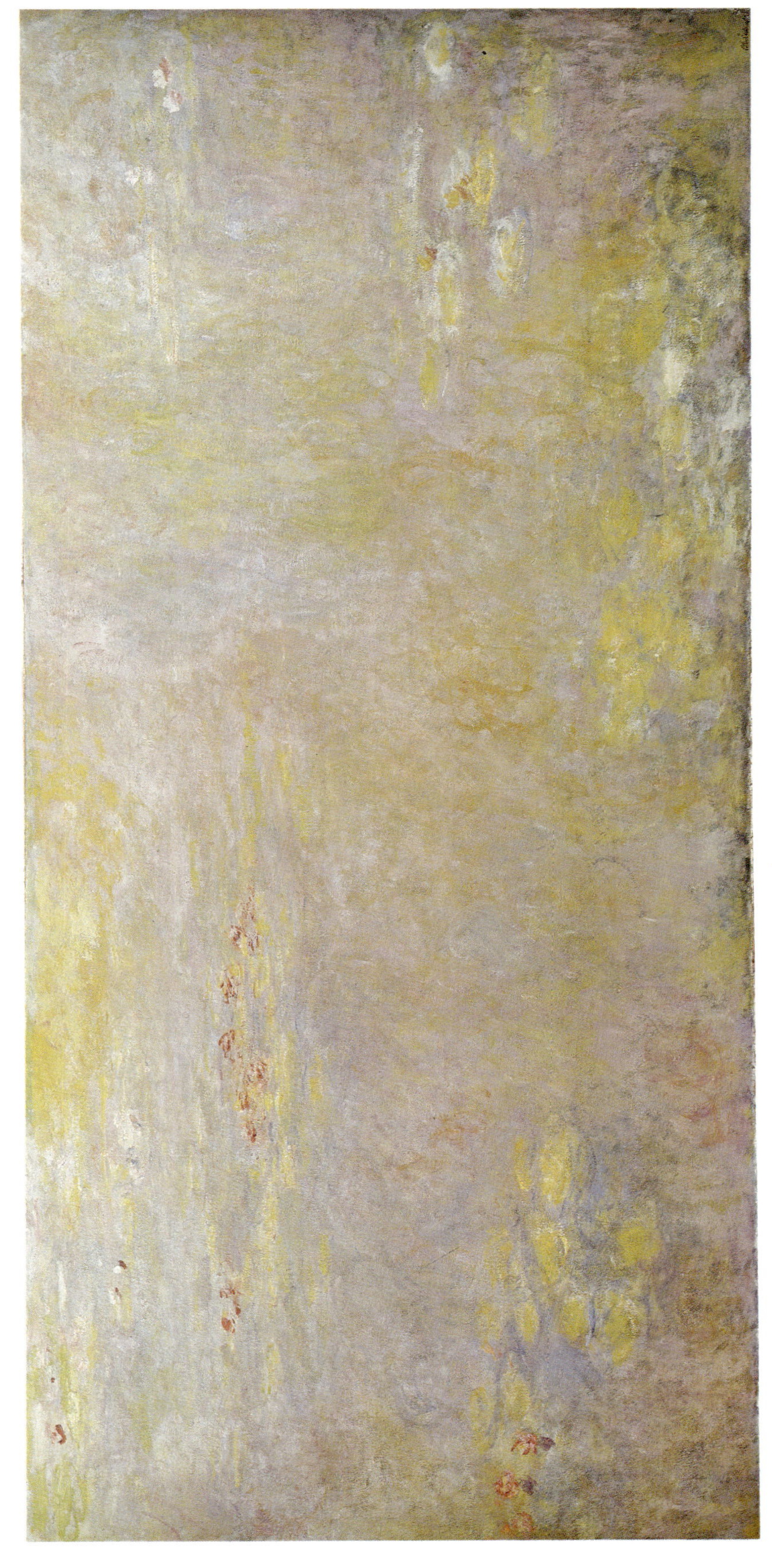

Index to Plates

Note : page numbers throughout refer to the position of the illustrations